HERESY

HERESY

A Novel

By FRANK SPINELLA

RESOURCE *Publications* · Eugene, Oregon

HERESY
A Novel

Copyright © 2014 Frank Spinella. All rights reserved. Except for brief quotations in critical publications or reviews, no part of this book may be reproduced in any manner without prior written permission from the publisher. Write: Permissions. Wipf and Stock Publishers, 199 W. 8th Ave., Suite 3, Eugene, OR 97401.

Resource Publications
An Imprint of Wipf and Stock Publishers
199 W. 8th Ave., Suite 3
Eugene, OR 97401

www.wipfandstock.com

ISBN 13: 978-1-62564-536-4

Manufactured in the U.S.A.

*"The Lord created me at the beginning of his work,
the first of his acts of long ago.
Ages ago I was set up,
at the first, before the beginning of the earth.
When there were no depths I was brought forth,
when there were no springs abounding with water.
Before the mountains had been shaped,
before the hills, I was brought forth—
when he had not yet made earth and fields,
or the world's first bits of soil."*

—Proverbs 8:22–26

Preface

For all that has been written about him, Arius remains a rather obscure figure in history. Few people today know anything more of him than that he was a fourth century Christian heretic, and perhaps that his heresy was the moving force behind the adoption of the Nicene Creed that, in a slightly modified form adopted a half-century later in Constantinople, nearly a billion worshippers still recite in church on a regular basis. Precisely because they are deemed heretical, Arius's teachings are presumed by most Christians—at least by most trinitarian Christians—to be unworthy of consideration. That his views must have been accepted by or at least attractive to a great many in the church of his time (would the Council of Nicaea have been convened otherwise?) likely never occurs to them. The harsh judgment of history has effectively squelched his antitrinitarian theology, and that is enough for the average believer; no need to consider how that theology came to be branded as heresy, or how what now passes for orthodoxy triumphed. Indeed, many are content simply to assign the Trinity to the category of unfathomable mystery. As Sir Isaac Newton once commented, "It is the temper of the hot and superstitious part of mankind in matters of religion ever to be fond of mysteries, and for that reason to like best what they understand least."

As one of those billion regular creed reciters, first as a Roman Catholic and later as an Episcopalian, I have always found the phrase "true God from true God, begotten not made, of one being (*homoousion*) with the Father" to be a rather vague expression of the nature of the Son of God, yet one whose meaning ought to be understood if it is to be recited as part of a profession of faith. Questions such as what "begotten" means in this context, and whether the Father and the pre-incarnate Son are two separate beings

Preface

or two expressions of a single undivided being, strike me as important ones to answer.

This novel was written on the premise that I am not alone in this view, that professions of faith are, for all of us, meaningful and valuable. Of what value is a profession of faith if its meaning is not understood by those professing it? I learned to recite a pledge of allegiance to the American flag by rote at the age of five, and could be forgiven for not appreciating its meaning then. But I am not five years old today.

At any age, memorizing a mantra inevitably shifts significance from the meaning of the words to the bare fact of their expression. Creeds can easily become mantras, which may explain why it is rare for Christians today to reflect on their beliefs about the nature of Jesus Christ and his relationship to the Father, even as they pledge them aloud. How far we have come from the state of affairs described by Saint Gregory of Nyssa, who wrote of Constantinople on the eve of that city's Council in 381 CE:

> Throughout the city everything is taken up by such discussions: the alleyways, the marketplaces, the broad avenues and city streets; the hawkers of clothing, the money-changers, those selling us food. If you ask about small change, someone would philosophize to you about the Begotten and Unbegotten. If you inquire about the price of bread, the reply comes: "The Father is greater and the Son is a dependent." If you should ask: "Is the bath prepared?" someone would reply, "The Son was created from not-being."

Indeed, such Arian notions had so permeated Christianity by this time that Saint Jerome lamented, with only mild exaggeration, that "the world awoke to find itself Arian." This was an era when people wore their religion on their sleeves and talked with each other about their beliefs regularly, to an extent nearly unfathomable today.

Burning issue it may have been then; but history is written by the winners, and the winners in the Arian controversy did their best to ensure that Arius's own writings, at least in their original imprint, would not survive to re-stir the controversy for future generations. Reliance on his detractors' accounts of what he taught necessarily makes researching Arius somewhat difficult and uncertain—but not impossible. What emerged from my own research was a man whose doctrine was essentially a conservative reaction to a liberal group of Alexandrian church fathers whose Platonist sentiments and allegorizing tendencies were getting the better of them.

Preface

Placing Arius as a conservative voice in a liberal era requires abandoning our modern notions of what is theologically conservative or liberal, notions colored by centuries of evolution in Christian theology, which in the West got something of a complete overhaul by Augustine just as the Arian controversy was dying down. The march of Christianity outward from Palestine into the Greek world inevitably resulted in a cultural and philosophical disconnect, as tales told and texts written from a Jewish/messianic perspective were being interpreted by men imbued in a Greek philosophical tradition. Those few scattered passages in the emerging New Testament canon that could arguably be deemed binitarian or (far less frequently) trinitarian yielded no coherent picture of the Son's participation in the Godhead, and two centuries of patristic thinking were occupied by the effort to weave that idea into a doctrine that was consistent with Scripture. It was thus natural that Greek philosophy, which had long sought to locate an ontological bridge between the One and the Many, between the realm of soul/spirit and the material world, would provide the looms for this tapestry. Particularly in Alexandria, Christianity was discovering its affinity with middle-Platonism and using it as a lens through which to view Christian concepts, furnishing the early church fathers with a template for reworking Jewish monotheism into a trinitarianism that could successfully resist devolving into tritheism.

If this seems somewhat foreign to us, it is because we are so far removed, theologically as well as temporally, from the early church fathers. For them, the conundrum of a melding of divine and human natures overshadowed the Incarnation's status as a necessary step in the plan of salvation. In Arius's time the manger rather than the cross was at the center of the theological roundtable; today that focus is reversed, due in no small part to the Reformation's hoisting of Paul's epistles, which point almost exclusively to Christ's death rather than his birth, up the masthead. By the time of the Reformation, the "problem" of Christ's dual nature was long since taken as solved. We cannot appreciate Arius in context today without sloughing off sixteen centuries of rather thick bark, and that is not easy to do.

It is even harder to put aside modern notions of "equality" and "identity," concepts that today have a mathematical tinge (if $F = G$ and $S = G$, then $S = F$), and adopt third-century Greek understandings of these concepts in order to see how Father and Son might both be thought of as God, and yet as distinct, without doing violence to the tenet that God is One. Some appreciation of this "higher" math is needed in order to set the Arian stage, and that takes a bit of effort for the modern mind—and not *just* the modern mind; many pre-Arian heresies, such as Adoptionism (which emphasized the Son's distinction from the Father) and Sabellianism (which emphasized their identicalness), arose because their adherents couldn't quite do the math here either. As the Latin apologist Tertullian bemoaned well over a century before Nicaea, "The simple, indeed (I will not call them unwise and unlearned) who always constitute the majority of believers, are startled at the dispensation (of the Three in One) . . . They are constantly throwing out against us that we are preachers of two gods and three gods."

This is hardly an unnatural reaction to Trinitarian teaching even for the wise and learned. Thinking of two beings as distinct, and yet as sharing the same substance or essence, the same *ousia*, presents no difficulty unless that substance or essence or *ousia* is itself the unique and absolute self-subsistence of the Mosaic "I AM"—for by definition only one being can have *that* as its essence. At least today we would see this as a definitional problem; then, it was viewed as a relational one. Efforts in Arius's time to solve the dilemma—and the first three centuries of the Christian era were marked by an astonishing array of such efforts—are best understood from this perspective.

I found my own thinking on all of this easier to explain in the form of a novel. Perhaps that was inevitable given that I am not a theologian. But I do think that when writing a novel on a theological subject, a lack of theological training is no disqualifier. Henry James, in his essay *The Art of Fiction*, attributes to the novelist the ability "to guess the unseen from the seen." James was not describing the essence of religious or theological study, but he may as well have been; for what other field of study is more engaged in precisely such a pursuit?

Moreover, because they are by nature indirect explications, stories have a capacity to stir the imagination that is not found in academic treatises. From earliest times stories have been the primary tools for conveying theological concepts, as was perhaps required by the subject matter, for which direct experience and thus direct language was lacking. This imaginative stirring has inevitably fostered greater understanding of the subject. The divine "story" was and is a collaborative one, told amongst ourselves again and again, augmented in imaginative ways. The use of story still serves that function.

This particular story would have been impossible without the encouragement of my wife, Linda. She *does* have theological training (a masters degree in divinity from Harvard), and if, at times, she has vaguely suspected that this book might have been an attempt to upstage her, I am confident that her suspicions are dispelled by the final product; such an attempt was clearly too feeble ever to be workable. I knew that all along. I dedicate this book to her.

Acknowledgments

Scripture quotations are from the *New Revised Standard Version Bible*, © 1989, Division of Christian Education of the National Council of the Churches of Christ in the U.S.A. Used by permission. All rights reserved.

Quotations from the Epistle of Barnabas, the Second Epistle of Clement, the writings of Ignatius, Theophilus, Irenaeus, Justin Martyr, Tertullian, Hippolytus, Clement of Alexandria, Dionysius of Alexandria, Gregory Thaumaturgus, Origen; the various letters of Alexander, Eusebius of Nicomedia and Constantine; the Edict of Milan; the Creed of Eusebius of Caesarea and his letter to his diocese after Nicaea are from *Ante-Nicene Fathers* (Roberts and Donaldson, eds.,1886), and *Nicene and Post-Nicene Fathers, Series II* (Schaff, et al., eds., 1890). Arius's letters to Alexander and to Eusebius of Nicomedia are taken from *Documents Illustrative of the History of the Church*, vol. II (Kidd, ed., 1923). Quotations from Philo are from Yonge, *The Works of Philo Judaeus* (1855), and those from Plotinus are from MacKenna and Page, *Plotinus: The Enneads* (rev. ed. 1930). Constantine's speech at Nicaea is taken from Schaff, *History of the Christian Church* (1884). The Nicene Creed itself is from R.P.C. Hanson's *The Search for the Christian Doctrine of God* (1988), used by permission. Quotation from *The Didache* is from Anthony Jones' *The Teaching of the Twelve* (2009), used by permission. The creed of the Synod of Antioch is from Rowan Williams' *Arius: Heresy and Tradition* (rev. ed. 2001), used by permission.

I owe a further debt to Rowan Williams for recommending Tim Vivian, Professor of Philosophy & Religious Studies at California State University Bakersfield, as a reviewer of the book. His helpful comments greatly improved it. Thanks are due as well to Joe Reidy, Adjunct Professor of History at Saint Louis University, for troubleshooting the novel's historical plausibility. Rarely did I ignore their suggestions, and always at my peril.

Chapter 1

She always arrives just before dusk, perching on the same branch, watching, waiting. Compared to other Pharaoh eagle-owls I have seen, she is on the smallish side, but with those piercing yellow-orange eyes that take everything in, missing nothing—including me. We have an understanding, she and I. It is simply this: we are to keep our respectful distance.

Several times have I seen her take flight, soaring with a grace that belies her deadly purpose. When she hunts for rodents in the failing light, she is awesome to watch: a silent, devastating dive toward her prey, seizing it with talons far too strong to permit any consideration of escape (as if her victim could consider anything at all in the shock of the moment), snatching it from the ground and up ever higher into the terrifying sky with the fearsome beating of her powerful wings.

But I do not come here to watch a hunter.

I come to pray. Here on the outskirts of Alexandria, on the western shore of Lake Mareotis, its cool waters fed by canals from the Nile, I pray aloud. I pray that God hears me. But what does he hear? Is it my words only, or the thoughts of my heart that words can but poorly express? Does he see in my heart a genuine desire to be submissive to his will, or only a conditional one, tempered by human frailty and restricted to that which is not too difficult, not too inconvenient? I know which. God sees all. More than this owl sees.

How hard it is to pray sincerely sometimes! All too often I find my words encumbered by other thoughts. Even when those words are divinely scripted, even as I pray as the Lord taught us to pray, I find that I cannot slow my mind from distractions. I pray aloud, "Thy will be done on earth,

Heresy

as it is in heaven," but I think to myself, is God's will not *always* done? Scripture reports that Job said to God, "I know that you can do all things, and that no purpose of yours can be thwarted." Doesn't that make it pointless to pray that God's will be done? Who can resist it? Yet I know that the Lord would never institute an irrelevancy. He wants us to desire the same things as God. He asks us to conform our wills to God's. And stilling the mind is always the first step toward discerning God's will.

I am young, and unskilled in the art of meditation. The cares of my world intrude, and weigh heavily on my shoulders—my studies at the Catechetical School, my secretarial service to the Bishop, my writing, my duties as a new deacon. Somehow I must find a way to cast them all aside for a moment. Here, now, sitting under this tree, I must put them out of mind and trust that God will call out to me. I know that he sees me sitting here. The way Jesus saw Nathanael sitting under the fig tree before Philip called out to him to "come and see" the son of Joseph from Nazareth. Nathanael got up, came and saw, saw that Jesus knew him already, knew there was no deceit in his heart; and Nathanael asked in bewilderment *how, how* did Jesus know him. "I saw you under the fig tree," was Jesus' simple answer. Nothing more. At once Nathanael replied with a declaration that defied all logic, a conclusion that could not rationally be drawn from Jesus' mere vision of him under the tree: "Rabbi, you are the Son of God!"

Jesus waits for my like reply. Will it form on my lips as readily as it did on Nathanael's? Will it rise up from my heart? "The word is near you, on your lips and in your heart," Paul wrote to the Romans. Let it be so!

And so I pray. I pray to confess in my heart that Jesus Christ is truly God, to *feel* its truth in the depths of my being. No mere intellectual assent to the conclusion, as though it were a geometrical proof distilled from undoubted axioms, will suffice here. No amount of study, whether of the Scriptures or of the writings of church fathers—all of which I have scrutinized extensively for many years—can yield the certainty I seek. That can come only from the Spirit. Inspiration, not logic, sparked Nathanael's conclusion, and must spark mine as well. If, as Paul declared to the Corinthians, "no one can say 'Jesus is Lord' except by the Holy Spirit," how much more is the Spirit's guidance needed for one to say "Jesus is *God*." How much more blessed are those who, not having seen, yet believe, and declare with Thomas that Jesus is "My Lord *and my God*."

At the Catechetical School many of my fellow deacons argue that Thomas' twofold declaration was redundant, that "Lord" and "God" are

Chapter 1

functionally equivalent. They point to the Hebrew Scriptures' use of the word "Lord" as a stand-in for the unutterable name of God, time and again—and they argue from this that Jesus' divinity must be entailed by his lordship. They quote David's Psalm, 'The Lord said to my lord, 'Sit at my right hand, until I make your enemies your footstool,'" and insist that David must have used "my lord" as a title of divinity. But the Hebrew word that the Greek renders as "my lord" is regularly employed to describe an earthly rather than a divine being. David is no exception; even after Saul anointed him king, David referred to Saul as "my lord." How, then, can we know whether "my lord" in his Psalm was intended to refer to a divine being or a human one?

I think of Simon Peter's quotation of the same Psalm when he proclaimed at Pentecost that "God has made him both Lord and Messiah, this Jesus whom you crucified," and wonder how the Jews who were converted that day understood his words. God made him *Lord*? Perhaps so; lordship can be granted or inherited. But God made him *God*? The very concept would have been almost unintelligible to any Jew! Surely Simon Peter, no less than the Jews in his audience, understood that "God" and "Lord" were not equivalent concepts. One refers to the Supreme Being; the other is simply an acknowledgement of sovereignty and dominion, equivalent to "master." The logical leap from "Jesus is Lord" to "Jesus is God" is as great as Nathanael's.

If anything, Simon Peter's words widen the logical gap for me. If God *made* him Lord, doesn't that suggest he was *not* Lord to begin with, and received power and glory only later as a reward for his obedience to the Father's will? Yet that is precisely what the fifty-third chapter of Isaiah implies: God allotted him "a portion with the great" for agreeing to die for our sins. Paul's Letter to the Philippians likewise teaches that "he humbled himself and became obedient to the point of death—even death on the cross. *Therefore* God also highly exalted him and gave him the name that is above every name." The Letter to the Hebrews is even more explicit, suggesting that Christ endured the cross "for the sake of the joy that was set before him," and now "has taken his seat at the right hand of the throne of God." And that is where Simon Peter's speech at Pentecost places him, "exalted at the right hand of God." But this notion of exalting Christ as a reward troubles me. After all, if he was truly God, he could not have been *made* Lord; that station would already have been his automatically, and not a reward for sacrifice. How could it be otherwise? Suppose the cup *had* passed him by; what would have happened *then*? An empty seat in the throne room of heaven?

Once again, I am being too analytical. I must find a way to halt this cascading river of rationalization running through my mind, before it deprives the day of its prayerful possibilities. Prayer is a contemplative journey, and like any other journey it requires preparation—but unlike physical journeys, this one requires us not to pack but to unpack. So much baggage! The gentle lapping of the lake at the shoreline soothes me as I strive to empty my mind of distractions and open myself to the Spirit, to the chance for inspiration, for insight. A soft breeze dances off the water, bending the tips of the reeds in the shallows; I inhale it deeply. Relaxing every part of my body, I close my eyes and breathe slowly, dispelling all thoughts until even my consciousness of waiting for insight is gone.

Suddenly what washes over me instead—or perhaps this *is* the insight—can only be described as a premonition, yet one so palpably real it is as though I am hearing Christ's words speaking to me aloud. They are words of warning:

There is danger approaching, Athanasius!

My eyes tighten shut even more; I hold my breath. Yes, Lord, I can sense something. I can feel it in the pit of my stomach, almost sickening me!

Someone is coming to attack us!

Yes, Lord; but who *is* it? Is a new persecution about to be mounted by Rome? No, somehow I sense that this is different. More insidious. My pulse races and my skin grows clammy. I try to concentrate, but the effort is self-defeating; the contours of this peril to the Faith become more elusive the more I try to bring it into focus, like a shadowy imperfection on the cornea, just off center, floating away as the eye vainly attempts to follow it and pull it back from the periphery. I cannot make it out clearly.

The cryptic warning fades as quickly as it arrived, and the wave of nausea passes. Still shaking, I exhale deeply, my quivering palms pushing beads of sweat from my brow up over my scalp. If infidels are truly arriving to storm the gates of Christ's kingdom, I will not be able to discern them today.

But perhaps it was nothing. Just as dreams can reveal either truth or fantasy, this might have been fantasy. One can all too easily mistake the surfacing of one's own latent fears for divine insight.

Chapter 1

Darkness overtakes the day. The owl soars somewhere above; I have lost sight of her. It is time to return to the city.

Chapter 2

Fifteen miles off the coast of Egypt, Arius peered excitedly through the darkness ahead of his ship, and could already see its glow in the distance. With its powerful reflective mirrors and a height of nearly three hundred cubits, the massive marble lighthouse on the eastern point of the island of Pharos had been guiding ships safely into the harbor of Alexandria for nearly six hundred years. Each time he caught sight of it, whether from land or from sea, by day or by night, Arius could not help but marvel at the wondrous structure, its intricate system of pulleys, gears and winches for hoisting firewood up the interior shaft to its summit rivaling the Pyramids themselves as a feat of engineering. He recalled vividly the first time he'd seen it, as a wide-eyed youth arriving in the great city from his native Libya. It was as impressive to him now as then, never becoming commonplace.

But tonight, Arius viewed the fire burning atop the magnificent beacon differently—as a torch of justice. Arius was returning from exile at the invitation of Achillas, the newly installed Bishop of Alexandria. A full year had passed since Achillas' predecessor Peter had excommunicated and banished Arius—retaliation, he was convinced, for his support of Melitius, the rival Egyptian bishop who had denounced Peter for fleeing the city during the Diocletian persecution. Melitius decried what he saw as Peter's cowardice; but for Arius it was Peter's intellectual dishonesty that gave greater offense. A shepherd who abandons his flock in its time of distress is indeed contemptible; but then to justify his flight by pointing to the words of Matthew's gospel, "*When they persecute you in one town, flee to the next*"—how utterly transparent! Would that Peter had read just a few verses further: "*Those who find their life will lose it, and those who lose their life for my*

Chapter 2

sake will find it." Was it any wonder that upon his return to Alexandria during a lull in the persecution, Peter had quickly insisted on amnesty for those who, under threat of torture, had renounced their faith to save their skins? But there would be no leniency extended to Arius. Surely a bishop who twists the gospel to his own purposes, Arius had preached to any who would listen, is unworthy of the rank. And for that ill-advised comment, he had permanently incurred Peter's wrath.

Yet it was Peter's announced excuse for excommunicating him, branding him a heretic for his theological views, that disgusted Arius the most. *Intellectual dishonesty yet again*, he thought. Peter may have redeemed himself from any charge of cowardice; reports had already spread beyond Egypt of his courageous martyrdom, assisting his guards in carrying out his sentence by showing them how to smuggle him out of the prison to avoid the throngs of his faithful who were rioting to block his execution. But to Arius, the bishop's redemption only lent credibility to his disingenuous decree. Peter was beloved by most Egyptian Christians, who might well consider his enemies as their enemies for that reason alone. That could prove to be a challenge, he thought. But for Arius tonight, leaning forward against the rail in the prow of the ship, no challenge seemed insurmountable.

His year away had been painful on many levels, yet Arius never lost hope that he would one day return. Now that Peter had gone on to his reward, new leadership promised greater tolerance in Alexandria, and Arius was anxious to test its limits. Quite a few free-thinking clerics throughout the Nile delta region had expressed some sympathy for his theological speculations, and he was grateful for that; but sympathy was a poor substitute for official recognition. Finally, he would now be restored to the legitimacy he craved. Ah, how sweet the taste of vindication! Since the moment Achillas' letter had arrived, Arius could barely keep another thought in his head apart from the possibilities unfolding before him. Within the month, he expected, he would be elevated by Achillas from deacon to presbyter, and if he was reading between the lines of Achillas' letter correctly, perhaps even given charge of Alexandria's oldest church in the waterfront district of Baucalis, one reputedly established by Saint Mark himself. And after that . . . who could say?

The importance of the task he was about to undertake was firmly etched in Arius's mind. His time of exile had opened his eyes to a harsh reality: Christianity throughout the Empire was splitting along theological lines to the point that its very foundation was being threatened. Sabellians argued with Monatists, and Novatians with both; factions of all sorts were everywhere undermining the faith. If its leaders continued to press their own disparate views on key theological points and did not adopt a consistent and defensible doctrine, the church would eventually founder from schisms, like a rudderless ship adrift in shallow waters. His old friend and mentor, Lucian of Antioch, had warned Arius of precisely this just before his execution in Nicomedia. That final night of his life, sitting soberly in his prison cell, he urged Arius to use his persuasive oratory skills as a tool for reform and unity. Do not waste your time debating with pompous bishops whose minds are not open to change, Lucian had counseled him; rather, preach the truth to the masses in simple terms, so that even the common believer can understand it. Work for change from the bottom up. Those who can reason for themselves do not want to be told what to believe; they want to trust in their own ability to understand the truth as rational beings. Make the Scriptures make sense, make *Christ* make sense, and the people will follow.

Now, at long last, an opportunity had come to put Lucian's sage advice into practice, and Arius was determined to make the most of it. There was no more fertile ground for cultivating his rationalist approach to Christian doctrine than Alexandria, the city of Euclid and Ptolemy, of Philo and Plotinus, of Clement and Origen, home to the greatest library in the world, attracting scholars and truth seekers from far and wide. If any city could lay claim to the intellectual legacy of ancient Athens, surely it was Alexandria. Even among the common folk, one was as apt to hear Greek as Coptic on its streets, as likely to hear discussion of philosophy as of politics. Here the Septuagint, in many ways the very bible of the Christian church, had been penned, and here Arius would make it understood and defend it against the metaphoric interpretations so much in vogue in recent years. Yes, *yes,* Arius thought with a smile as he inhaled the cool, briny air and watched the distant glow of the lighthouse steadily increase in intensity, along with his excitement. The intellectual climate would be perfect for reception of his message.

He had no way of knowing that twelve hundred miles away, at that precise moment, a favorable change in the political climate was about to begin as well.

Chapter 3

Like any general whose army had performed admirably in battle, Constantine was cautiously optimistic. Despite leaving half of his forces along the Rhine to protect the Empire's northern frontier, his civil war against Maxentius, his brother-in-law and rival for supremacy in the West, had thus far been going as smoothly as he could have hoped. Descending into Italy from the north, he encountered no resistance coming through the Alps, and was barely challenged by the loyalist forces stationed in the Piedmont foothills. A successful siege of the walled city of Segusium followed, and with the victory he ordered his troops to refrain from the usual plundering in order to court favor with the locals. "This is a war to liberate Rome, not to occupy it," he told them.

The strategy worked. Word of Constantine's leniency spread to the civilian populace ahead of his advancing legions, and when Maxentius' garrisons at Turin marched out of the city to engage Constantine's forces, its citizens barricaded the gates behind them, cutting off any retreat and forcing Maxentius' soldiers to fight with their backs to the city walls. Their surrender quickly followed. Milan fell in a similar fashion, Parma soon afterwards, and then Modena and Bologna. Rome lay ahead. Constantine knew that Maxentius would defend it to the death. But would he remain in his well-fortified capital and try to repel the invasion from within its walls, or would he lead his army across the Tiber and carry the fight to his enemy?

The answer soon came back from Constantine's scouts: Maxentius' forces, significantly larger than Constantine's, had already advanced their defensive position across the river at the Milvian Bridge and destroyed it behind them, setting in its place a makeshift pontoon bridge out of boats bolted together, over which his troops could retreat if necessary and then quickly disassemble behind them to hinder pursuit. But the decisive battle would be fought on this side of the Tiber.

Constantine dismissed the scouts and gazed up into the brilliant afternoon October sky, pondering his next move. Suddenly he had a strange and captivating vision; etched into the sky just above the sun, he saw clearly the imprint of a cross, the symbol of the Christians. He squinted, shielding his eyes with his forearm, and looked again, as directly as he could bear. *Still there!* When he closed his eyes the bright image remained, slowly fading but unmistakably emblazoned in shadowy relief against the insides of his eyelids. Opening them, he saw it anew, this time even more distinctly, until the searing sunlight again forced him to look away. Surely this must portend *some*thing, he thought—but *what*? Constantine was no Christian, although he had a measure of respect for the religion and its power over the minds of men; early in his military career he had seen many Christians willingly go to their deaths rather than sacrifice to other gods. His mother and stepmother were both Christian sympathizers, and had occasionally tried to interest him in learning more about the faith, but he had always rebuffed them. Now, he was presented with something he could not dismiss, something full of portent, a sign in need of interpretation.

Constantine summoned his officers and asked if they had seen the celestial cross; none said they had. Despite their quizzical looks, their lack of corroboration did nothing to shake his certainty in what he had witnessed. It puzzled him greatly, distracting his focus from the plan of attack that he and his officers were busily putting together for the following morning.

That night as he slept fitfully in his tent, Constantine received his answer. In a dream, he saw superimposed against each other the Greek letters *chi* and *rho*, the first two letters of *Christos*, and heard a booming voice which he took to be that of Christ himself, saying *"In hoc signo vinces"*—"By this sign you shall conquer." The voice commanded him to inscribe the Chi-Rho symbol on his soldiers' shields before going into battle. Constantine awoke, shaking and in a sweat, but determined to follow the divine instruction.

At dawn he summoned his officers, directing them to do as the dream had commanded, and within the hour hundreds of his soldiers' shields bore in charcoal the Christogram that came to be known as the *Labarum*:

As he prepared for battle, and for the first time in his life, Constantine prayed to the Christian God: "Bring me this victory, and henceforth I shall worship none but you!"

Chapter 3

By mid morning the two armies were fully engaged, Constantine himself leading one of the cavalry wings, the sign of *Christos* inscribed on his helmet. Constantine's troops fought that day with a ferocity that put the defenders on their heels. His cavalry from the flanks and his infantry from the center relentlessly pressed Maxentius' forces back toward the Tiber, which denied them the room to fall back and regroup, resulting in disorganization that gave the advantage to the invading army. As Maxentius' cavalry was overwhelmed and his heavy infantry found itself pinned down, panic began to set in—for in destroying the Milvian Bridge, they had hindered their own retreat! Maxentius' Praetorian Guard fought valiantly to the last man on the banks of the river, while his remaining troops rushed madly onto the pontoon bridge until it collapsed helplessly into the water. Maxentius himself drowned in the Tiber while attempting to escape, unable to swim the current in his heavy armor.

By nightfall what was left of the defending army had surrendered. Constantine's victory was complete. When Maxentius' body was found washed up on the river bank the next morning, his head was promptly mounted on a spear, and the victorious army marched into Rome with it that afternoon, a triumphant and elated Constantine leading the procession to the Capitoline Hill. He knew that the Senate was prepared to accept whoever emerged as victor, but the hearty cheers of the throngs of Romans lining the streets eight and ten deep gave him even more certainty that unity and stability would now come to the western empire—*his* empire.

Constantine kept the solemn bargain he had made prior to battle at the Milvian Bridge; he prayed in fervent thanksgiving to a God he did not know, convinced that he owed his victory to the protection of Christ. Although not then choosing to be baptized, he soon began to study in earnest the religion that had suffered such persecution at the hands of his predecessors.

Six months later he and Licinius, the Emperor of the eastern empire who had made the trip from Nicomedia to Milan in order to marry Constantine's half-sister Constantina in a display of political unity, would sign

Heresy

the Edict of Milan, extending freedom of worship to Christians everywhere and directing provincial magistrates to restore them their property:

> "And accordingly we give you to know that, without regard to any provisos in our former orders to you concerning the Christians, all who choose that religion are to be permitted, freely and absolutely, to remain in it, and not to be disturbed in any ways, or molested. And we thought fit to be thus special in the things committed to your charge, that you might understand that the indulgence which we have granted in matters of religion to the Christians is ample and unconditional; and perceive at the same time that the open and free exercise of their respective religions is granted to all others, as well as to the Christians. For it befits the well-ordered state and the tranquility of our times that each individual be allowed, according to his own choice, to worship the Divinity; and we mean not to derogate aught from the honor due to any religion or its votaries.
>
> "Moreover, with respect to the Christians, we formerly gave certain orders concerning the places appropriated for their religious assemblies; but now we will that all persons who have purchased such places, either from our exchequer or from anyone else, do restore them to the Christians, without money demanded or price claimed, and that this be performed peremptorily and unambiguously; and we will also, that they who have obtained any right to such places by form of gift do forthwith restore them to the Christians: reserving always to such persons, who have either purchased for a price, or gratuitously acquired them, to make application to the judge of the district, if they look on themselves as entitled to any equivalent from our beneficence. All those places are, by your intervention, to be immediately restored to the Christians. And because it appears that, besides the places appropriated to religious worship, the Christians did possess other places, which belonged not to individuals, but to their society in general, that is, to their churches, we comprehend all such within the regulation aforesaid, and we will that you cause them all to be restored to the society or churches, and that without hesitation or controversy: Provided always, that the persons making restitution without a price paid shall be at liberty to seek indemnification from our bounty. In furthering all such things for the benefit of the Christians, you are to use your utmost diligence, to the end that our orders be speedily obeyed, and our gracious purpose in securing the public tranquility promoted."

Chapter 4

"'... In furthering all such things for the benefit of the Christians, you are to use your utmost diligence, to the end that our orders be speedily obeyed, and our gracious purpose in securing the public tranquility promoted.'"

When Alexander finished reading his just-acquired Greek translation of the Edict to the incredulous priests and deacons gathered before him in the great hall of the Alexandrian library, they could barely contain their exuberance. Cries of praise to God reverberated throughout the euphoric room. Watching them embrace each other, Alexander waited for the excitement to dissipate a bit before holding up his hands, palms outward, signifying that the clergy should restrain themselves and be silent once more.

"My brothers in Christ," Alexander continued in Coptic with all the passion he could muster, "God has truly shown favor upon his faithful, and it is fitting that we give thanks. I therefore decree that tomorrow shall be a day of prayer and fasting in all of the churches throughout the city. It is regrettable that my predecessor, blessed Achillas, did not live to see this day, for his joy would have been boundless. And mindful of the honor that you have bestowed upon me in choosing me as your bishop, I pledge to all of you that I will work tirelessly to make the most of this opportunity to spread the gospel, now that it may be received and practiced by all without fear of persecution. I pray that each of you will rededicate yourself to the task as well."

The chorus of solemn amens that rose from the gathering immediately gave way to renewed cheers and celebratory embraces. Even the usually staid Alexander could not suppress a broad grin as he clasped the shoulders and shook the hands of those nearest him. Then, across the noisy room, he spotted Arius, taller than the rest and difficult to miss, wearing the sleeveless tunic of the peripatetic philosophers that had become his trademark. The smile quickly left Alexander's face. When their eyes met, Arius nodded coolly in acknowledgement, and promptly turned away to resume conversing with his jubilant colleagues. Alexander pressed his way through the boisterous crowd toward the priest, casually acknowledging others as he passed, but with more than a hint of preoccupation.

When he reached Arius, the two men hesitated for a brief awkward moment before embracing without emotion and quickly separating. "Come to my study room, Arius," the bishop requested. "I would like to have a word with you." Arius excused himself from the small group that surrounded him and followed dutifully.

Closing the door to the reveling behind them, Alexander sized up his priest with a keen eye, searching for any hint of defiance in his demeanor. The two had been rivals for the bishopric of Alexandria, and although Arius had been a presbyter for only a short time, the wide support he had garnered, a tribute to his charisma and rhetorical skill, had taken Alexander by surprise. In the end, Arius bowed out of the running, to Alexander's great relief. But the strong following that Arius had garnered so quickly was still viewed by Alexander with suspicion, perhaps even a tinge of jealousy despite his office. This was not lost on Arius.

As he waited for the prelate to speak, Arius glanced at the Greek manuscript resting on the reading stand next to him, and immediately recognized the Second Epistle of Clement from its opening line: *"Brethren, it is fitting that you should think of Jesus Christ as of God. . ."* Had Alexander summoned him for a theological lecture? Surely this was not the time for esoteric debate! On a joyous day such as this, Arius thought to himself, we should be engaged in expressions of thankfulness, not argument.

"I have heard reports of the sermon you gave in Baucalis last week on the resurrection," the bishop began as he reached for an earthen jug and filled two cups with wine. "Quite interesting; and by all accounts very perceptive. I can't tell you how pleased I am to learn that you are not an Adoptionist, like Paul of Samosata and his pupil Lucian." He handed one of the cups to Arius, who accepted it but did not drink.

Arius felt himself being baited, but could not let the slur on his mentor's name go unchallenged. "Lucian was no Adoptionist. You know that."

"Do I? In any event, I'd like a copy of the sermon, if you wrote it out. A most scholarly exegesis of the opening verses of Paul's Epistle to the

Chapter 4

Romans, from what I understand. And challenging verses they are! I'm told you conceded the Adoptionists' point that *horisthentos* in the fourth verse should be translated as "appointed" or "installed" rather than as "declared," a translation which they proclaim as proof that Christ was *appointed* the Son of God at his resurrection, as opposed to having his preexisting sonship simply declared or affirmed by his resurrection. But then you proceeded to refute those who argue for Christ's exaltation to sonship only at his resurrection; or at his transfiguration; or even at his baptism. 'He who did not withhold his *own* son,' you quoted from later in the epistle, surely must have had a proper son all along rather than an adopted one; wasn't that how you put it? A masterful defense of Christ's preincarnate sonship! It is no wonder that you have gained such a following in so short a time, Arius. You have quite a gift."

When Arius made no response, Alexander's tone grew stern. "And you should take better care not to use that gift to sow dissention. If you have an issue with what others preach, I suggest you take it up with them privately first. Especially *me*! Criticizing my sermon on the Trinity, and even accusing me of Sabellianism; was that designed to endear yourself to me? You should pick your fights more carefully, Arius! Do not forget who was chosen to shepherd this flock, and who is charged with protecting it from ravenous wolves coming down from the hills—or from Libya!"

Arius remained expressionless, hiding his indignation at this bald attack on his character. Alexander, however, could not hide his chagrin at Arius's lack of reaction; his face reddened in anger and his eyes narrowed menacingly. "Know this, my priest: just before his death, Peter warned both Achillas and me that your views were unorthodox, even dangerous, and that you should not be sanctioned to preach. Achillas nevertheless saw fit to ordain you. I am not sure I would have, either then or now. We shall see what we shall see. Tread lightly, preacher! I have my eye on you." Alexander raised his cup to his lips and drained it with a single swallow, his defiant eyes never looking away from Arius as he tilted his head back.

"You have no cause for concern," Arius replied calmly, again repressing the outrage he felt. "I am obedient to my bishop. Will that be all? I am anxious to return to Baucalis and share today's good tidings with my congregation."

"Go," Alexander commanded in frustration. Still emotionless, Arius placed his unsipped cup of wine on the table, and with a slight perfunctory bow to the prelate, turned and proceeded toward the door, giving a quick sideways look at the Clementine manuscript as he passed. *Never*, he vowed to himself as he read its first line again.

Chapter 5

In mid-summer, when the rains do not come and the air is still, the foul and pungent smells of the crowded city streets can be nauseating. I breathe shallowly through my mouth as I hurry along to noon prayers with the other deacons.

Crouched in the meager shade of the date trees near the entrance of the Catechetical School are the beggars, haggard and emaciated, who look upon the passing clerics first with entreating gazes of expectation, and then, disappointed, with such hatred and vituperation as to send a shudder up the spine of the most hardened. It is as though they feel entitled to receive bread from our hands. Bread, the ancient means of subsistence for the common throngs who press daily into the marketplace, was first baked here in Egypt thousands of years ago, and soon spread throughout the world as a staple of daily consumption. But for these supplicants in the street, bread may be theirs only by theft or by others' grace—and we deacons are the perceived dispensers of that grace, for they know the Christian teaching on love of neighbor and dispensing of charity to others. They know as well that we pass this way at midday, and it is from us particularly that they expect the charity that will quell the rumbling in their bellies. But today I have no bread, and I do not stop, nor even slow to apologize as I avert my eyes from theirs, carrying my guilt into the communal prayer hall.

The Apostle Paul admonished that we are to pray without ceasing, but this is not possible, except perhaps as Origen wrote: "*He prays without ceasing who combines prayer with right actions, and becoming actions with prayer. For the saying 'pray without ceasing' can only be accepted by us as a possibility if we may speak of the whole life of a saint as one great continuous prayer.*" Today, once again, that is not me. The beggars know.

Origen once studied in these very halls, where now I study him. I struggle mightily to understand him. The enigmatic Origen, who took so much in the Scriptures as allegorical, yet took literally the nineteenth chapter of Matthew regarding those who make themselves eunuchs for the sake of the kingdom of heaven! What monstrous insight could have inspired him to pick up a knife and castrate himself? It is said that later in life he regretted doing so. Male sexual function was an ancient prerequisite to communal worship; it is written in Deuteronomy, "No one whose testicles are crushed or whose penis is cut off shall be admitted to the assembly of the Lord." Yet Isaiah writes: "For thus says the Lord: To the eunuchs who keep my Sabbaths, who choose the things that please me and hold fast my covenant, I will give, in my house and within my walls, a monument and a name better than sons and daughters; I will give them an everlasting name that shall not be cut off." The two passages seem so inconsistent to me. Could it be that God changed his mind on this? No, no, I refuse to believe such a thing possible; it is written in the twenty-third chapter of Numbers that "God is not a human being, that he should lie, or a mortal, that he should change his mind." Yes, surely that must be right. It is solely a trait of humans to change their minds—as Origen, they say, changed his. A bit too late.

If celibacy is indeed the noble calling in the service of God that the Apostle Paul claims, castration is actually the coward's way out, preventing even the spontaneous sexual arousal that sometimes arises without the slightest visual stimulation or indulged fantasy. Many of the deacons have vowed to renounce the pleasures of the flesh—I have myself—but where would be the daily sacrifice, where the glory of resistance to temptation, if the experience of temptation were itself rendered impossible with a single swipe of the blade? A forced virgin is no virgin at all. The young maidens of the city who dedicate themselves to the service of the Lord know this. Their virginity is their glory because it is their constant choice.

It is nothing short of remarkable that so many of these young women—about seven hundred, by some accounts—have made an additional choice; they have attached themselves to the parish of Baucalis, where the Libyan presbyter Arius has thoroughly captivated the minds of the congregation with his sleek oratorical style. To me, Arius is as enigmatic as Origen, if not more so. The man is not overly flamboyant in his preaching,

Chapter 5

yet his charisma is as undeniable as his teaching is questionable. Alexander does not trust him. I have yet to make up my own mind, and prefer to give him the benefit of the doubt. Unlike some who have adopted an ascetic life style with unabashed fervor in recent years as though it were a surrogate for martyrdom in the new post-persecution era, Arius's asceticism appears genuine; he makes no great show of it, withdraws when he fasts, shows temperance and moderation in his habits. He is prayerful and serene, at least in public persona. Still, to surround himself with so many virgins carries at least a hint of impropriety, if not scandal. Alexander half-jokingly refers to them as "the harbor harem," and while his priests and deacons chuckle politely at the joke, no evidence has ever been brought forward to suggest any lack of chastity on Arius's part. If he has taken a consort from among these women, it has not even reached the rumor stage. Speculation and suspicion provide no basis for official reprobation, and none has been forthcoming. That is as it should be. There is enough in Arius's teachings to be concerned about without getting worked up over his alluring entourage.

And concern over his teaching is growing. Reports of his preaching hint at unorthodox theological leanings, particularly in regard to the divinity of Christ. He refers to the paradox of simultaneous unity and distinction, the one arising from a communication of divine substance from Father to Son, the other arising from subordination and inferiority of Son to Father. He regularly questions the possibility of an indivisible God generating a perfect image of himself without thereby becoming divisible. His sermons are replete with rationalist arguments rather than faith-based teachings. When he expounds on the Scriptures, it is with a bent toward the literal, which he then presses to the logical limits of textual meaning, cautioning his listeners against expansion beyond those limits. Yet, always, there is ambiguity and uncertainty in his message, particularly at the crucial point of affirming or denying the Son's full and co-equal divinity with the Father that has long formed part of our tradition. And so his views on the subject remain shrouded in mystery, albeit the subject of considerable speculation here among the catechumens.

Arius does not frequent the School, nor do I venture regularly to the harbor. Those few brief occasions when we have spoken have yielded no theologically intense discussions, yet he impressed me with his keen intelligence and careful choice of words. Though he is a presbyter and I a deacon, and though he is more than twice my age, his melancholy eyes show no trace of condescension or impatience. The man is difficult to read, and even

Heresy

more difficult to draw into debate; he chooses his skilful rhetorical forays carefully. Once, when I sought to engage him by asking his opinion on Origen's view that Christ's baptism in the Jordan revealed the Trinity through the simultaneous presence of Father, Son and Holy Spirit, he deflected the inquiry deftly: "I will defer to Christ's own interpretation of the event, in the synagogue in Nazareth, where Luke reports that Christ read from the sixty-first chapter of Isaiah and then announced the prophecy fulfilled in himself. May God's spirit descend upon you and anoint you for service as well, Athanasius. I pray that it may be so." Thoroughly disarmed, I could think of no response. Another time, I inquired if he would consider reviewing a chapter in the thesis I am writing on the Incarnation of the Word. He simply asked, "Do you follow John in concluding that 'the Word became flesh,' or do you go further and state, as John was careful *not* to do, that 'the Word became *man*?' For a man is more than flesh; he has a soul—a *human* soul. Do you posit in Christ a human soul, Athanasius, or a divine one?" Once again I could muster no answer, and simply shrugged, turning away in embarrassment at my inability to engage on the question.

Arius does more than bring home to me the reality of my own intellectual shortcomings. He scratches at the vulnerable space where I hide my doubts, where I encase the questionable elements and troubling entailments of the positions I stake out and strive to defend. He challenges my beliefs at their soft points.

The noon prayers are ended, but I linger to reflect quietly by myself. And for the beggars to disperse.

Chapter 6

Throughout the Mediterranean world as the Edict of Milan was put into practice, the spread of Christianity reached a pace it had not enjoyed in decades. Wholly apart from the cessation of persecutions, Constantine's own conversion had given the religion increased credibility, and it expanded steadily along with his hegemony. He saw in it a potential for unifying the empire, if only it could overcome its own internal squabbling, which seemed to the Emperor to be on the rise. In a perverse and ironic way, he deemed himself partially responsible for the increased dissention, for he knew that the cessation of Roman oppression had dissolved a significant bond of Christian unity: resistance against a common foe.

In the Egyptian capital, Arius devoted himself not only to preaching but to study, quietly spending as much time as possible at the ancient Temple of Serapis, where an offshoot of the city's great library was housed. There in the quiet of its marbled reading room, surrounded by thousands of scrolls catalogued to every field of human knowledge, he felt at home. His scholarly mind pored over the Scriptures and the writings of Greek philosophers and Christian thinkers, constantly formulating, discarding, revising and re-formulating his theories—all the while engaged in prayer and living the pious and ascetic lifestyle that had been his hallmark since returning to the city. Beyond the library walls his popularity grew steadily, as Christians from throughout the city and visitors from afar flocked to his church to hear sermons that expounded a more literal reading of Scripture, subtly challenging the allegorical interpretations that had marked Alexandrian thought for over a century and were regularly preached by the priests and catechumens who enjoyed Alexander's patronage. That Arius did not enjoy the prelate's favor had proven to be no obstacle at all to the growth of his adoring congregation, now by far the largest in the city.

Convinced that his popularity would be his protection, Arius grew ever bolder in his preaching. On a balmy Sunday morning, as early clouds gave way to brilliant sunshine, he stood outside of his church and greeted the many regular worshippers and inquisitive new visitors who had come to pray and to hear his words. As the crowd gathered, Arius felt an overwhelming sense of responsibility. There had been enough equivocation, enough innuendo in his sermons, enough laying a foundation for the conclusion he now felt ready to lay out. Ascending the pulpit to preach and looking out onto the throngs assembled before him, he knew that Alexander had spies among the congregation, but he was undeterred. Lucian had spent years making critical revisions of the text of the Septuagint to correct its Alexandrian colloquialisms. Now, this morning, Arius set himself to ridding it of the distinctly Alexandrian spin which rendered so much of it as an allegorical witness to Christ, no matter how strained the interpretation. The time had arrived.

"Be on your guard, my brothers and sisters," he preached in Coptic, "for we must test and prove everything in Scripture, lest we fall prey to the seductive attraction of mystical symbolism. There is unavoidable uncertainty in the allegorical interpretation of Scripture, and any retreat from what the words naturally convey to what furthers the interests of the interpreter is suspect, and a reason for caution. Origen, in his great work *Against Celsus*, accuses his adversary of falling 'into the most vulgar of errors, in supposing that in the law and the prophets there is not a meaning deeper than that afforded by a literal rendering of the words.' But I say to you, the Scriptures were written so that *all* of God's people might understand their message, not just a few; for what god would commission his lawgivers to render ambiguous statutes, or his prophets to obscure rather than to reveal?

"Yet false symbolism is all around us, and its adherents dispense it as though it were wisdom imparted to the elect. Let me read but one example, from the *Epistle of Barnabas* that was written two centuries ago here in Alexandria, a letter that Clement himself accorded the status of authoritative Scripture:

> 'Learn then, my children, concerning all things richly, that Abraham, the first who enjoined circumcision, looking forward in spirit to Jesus, practiced that rite, having received the mysteries of the three letters. For [the Scripture] saith, 'And Abraham circumcised ten, and

eight, and three hundred men of his household.' What, then, was the knowledge given to him in this? Learn the eighteen first, and then the three hundred. The ten and the eight are thus denoted — Ten by I, and Eight by H. You have [the initials of the name of] Jesus. And because the cross was to express the grace [of our redemption] by the letter T, he says also, "Three Hundred." He signifies, therefore, Jesus by two letters, and the cross by one. He knows this, who has put within us the engrafted gift of His doctrine. No one has been admitted by me to a more excellent piece of knowledge than this, but I know that ye are worthy.'

"Let us leave aside the fact that the quotation is spurious; for nowhere does the Book of Genesis declare that Abraham circumcised 318 men! The encryption here is rather obvious: the letters 'Iota' and 'Eta' are the tenth and eighth letters of the Greek alphabet, and are the first two letters of *Iēsous*; while the letter 'Tau' represents the number 300, and stands for the cross.

"No doubt Barnabas thought himself quite ingenious, when in fact he should have been quite embarrassed; Genesis was written in Hebrew, not Greek! This is the same error decried by the esteemed bishop Irenaeus, who wrote more than a century ago of the folly of 'transferring the name *Jesus*, which belongs to another language, to the numeration of the Greeks.' But while Abraham could hardly have 'received the mysteries of the three letters' in Greek, Barnabas' readers were familiar only with the Septuagint, so it was rather easy for him to foist this gematrial nonsense on the unwary.

"Yet what is most telling in this passage is the author's claimed imparting of this special 'knowledge' to the 'worthy.' Only to the chosen ones is the 'secret' mystery revealed; nothing is divulged to the uninitiated. And who among us would not wish to be numbered among the 'elect' and therefore somehow special and favored? Do not be fooled, my brothers and sisters. We are *all* worthy of receiving the truth! And the only 'secret' is that those who perpetuate such mystical foolishness are themselves far from the truth."

Arius could tell that his words were resonating with his listeners, as most of them nodded approvingly. Only a few in the crowd shifted uncomfortably. Did Alexander's spies realize he was speaking of them? How could they *not*? Just as the Pharisees knew when Christ's thinly veiled parables warned the crowds to beware of the teachers of that time, so too *they* knew now. But it did not matter; Arius could hold back no longer. It was time to plant the seed:

Heresy

"My friends, we must guard as well against interpretations that press the meaning of Scripture beyond what is supported by the text. Consider Christ's declaration in John's gospel, 'Very truly I tell you, before Abraham was, I am.' Some see in this a reference to the Mosaic "I AM WHO I AM," rendered *ego eimi ho ōn* in the Greek of the Septuagint, the Greek that Christ never spoke. John writes in Greek, and quotes only the *ego eimi*, only the 'I am,' and not the *ho ōn*, 'the One who is,' 'the Being,' 'the existent One.' According to John, Christ never used these additional words that designate the very name of God; yet, we are told by our preachers, he meant to imply them. Surely, they tell us, Christ would have simply said 'I was' rather than 'I am' if he meant the reference only temporally. Surely, they assert, the Jews who were prepared to stone him for this pronouncement correctly understood him as making a blasphemous declaration of divinity. My brothers and sisters, we must resist such speculations. There is a claim here of pre-existence, to be sure; but that is not the same as claiming to be God! It is, in truth, claiming no more than to be the first-born of God. Thus does the venerable Justin Martyr describe the pre-existent Christ as 'distinct from Him who made all things,' 'first power after God,' 'the first-born of God.'

"And so it is that we must ask ourselves how Christ can be, as the Apostle Paul wrote to the Colossians, 'the first-born of all creation,' *unless he himself was created*. And if created, in what sense can he be thought of as God?"

There! The challenge was laid down; there could be no turning back now.

Chapter 7

Out of breath and sweating profusely, Athanasius had literally run the entire sweltering distance from Baucalis to the bishop's residence, demanding an immediate audience. This news, he knew, could not wait.

The color drained from Alexander's face as he received his excited pupil's report of Arius's sermon, virtually word for word. Athanasius had that kind of memory, and a keen intellect to go with it. When his prize student had finished, Alexander exhorted him to sit and rest, and then paced slowly around the room, nervously stroking his beard. "I knew this day was coming, and feared it greatly. It is just as Paul warned in his letter to Timothy: *'For the time is coming when people will not put up with sound doctrine, but having itching ears, they will accumulate for themselves teachers to suit their own desires, and will turn away from listening to the truth and wander away to myths.'* We must stop that wandering before the flock is lost. How do you suggest we respond to this heresy? Should we engage Arius in public debate?"

"That is a possibility, to be sure," the young deacon responded, elated that Alexander was seeking his opinion. "But one fraught with risk. Arius was shrewd to use Justin Martyr as his foil today. He knows that if we rely on Justin's distinction between the immanent *Logos* and the expressed *Logos*, between an idea in the mind of God and the speech which expresses that idea, he can fall back on many of Justin's writings that support his own theories, pointing out Justin's own distinction between God and God's subordinate *Logos*."

Alexander nodded in agreement as he paced around the room, still tugging at his beard. "Right. Then we will simply ignore Justin, and condemn Arius's teachings as excluded by John's gospel, which casts Christ as the *Logos*, and the *Logos* as God."

Athanasius was more circumspect. "A public discussion of the nuances of the *Logos* is one I think we may wish to avoid, my bishop. Arius is masterful at exploiting double meanings, and will do so with *Logos*' double meaning of Word and Reason. No doubt Reason always existed with God, but the unlearned will naturally assume that God's Word emanates from Him at a particular time—and Arius will quickly enmesh us anew in debating Justin Martyr's immanence/expression dichotomy. I am concerned about affording him any opportunity to focus attention on this."

"I see no reason to fear any double meaning here," Alexander replied, "as long as Arius concedes that one meaning of *Logos* is indeed as the Wisdom of God, '*preceding the Word which announces her*,' as Origen put it in his commentary on John's Gospel. The Book of Wisdom refers to her as '*a reflection of eternal light, a spotless mirror of the working of God, and an image of his goodness.*' Surely reflections and images co-exist at all times with their sources, do they not?"

"Arius can make the opposite case rather easily," Athanasius rejoined in a respectful tone. "The verse you quote is immediately preceded by a reference to Wisdom as '*a breath of the power of God, and a pure emanation of the glory of the Almighty,*' which Arius will argue are manifestations that, like breath itself, issue at a given point in time rather than eternally. Worse, there are passages in Scripture which he can quote as proofs that Wisdom was *not* eternally co-existent. Consider the twenty-fourth chapter of Sirach, which likewise states that Wisdom '*came forth from the mouth of the Most High,*' but then recites that '*the Creator of all things gave me a command, and my Creator chose the place for my tent,*' and also '*Before the ages, in the beginning, he created me, and for all the ages I shall not cease to be.*' If we go down this path, Arius will quickly trap us and cut off any retreat except for the one he knows we do not wish to take: defending the Sabellian proposition that there is no distinction between creator and creature."

"Perhaps he will try. But he cannot deny that the Fourth Gospel quotes Christ as acknowledging that '*the Father and I are one.*' Where is his retreat from *that*?"

"An easy retreat, my bishop. The Fourth Gospel quotes Christ as using the same word 'one' when he prays '*Holy Father, protect them in your name that you have given me, so that they may be one, as we are one.*' And again, '*I ask not only on behalf of these, but also on behalf of those who will believe *in me through their word, that they may all be one. As you, Father, are in me and I am in you, may they also be in us, so that the world may believe that you have sent me. The glory that you have given me I have given them, so that they may be one, as we are one.*' If Christ used the word 'one' to describe the relationship between himself and his disciples, and indeed the relationship among all believers, it follows that the sense of 'one' used here by John's gospel cannot be that of identicalness in substance or being. Are we all gods? That is precisely the retreat Christ himself took when the Jews prepared to stone him for his comment that *'the Father and I are one.'* So will Arius."

"Then we will do battle with Arius on his own terms, and show that two things can be distinct, yet still share a common nature. When Dionysius was bishop in this city many years ago, he explained it quite well:

> *'The plant that springs from the root is something distinct from that whence it grows up; and yet it is of one nature with it. And the river which flows from the fountain is something distinct from the fountain. For we cannot call either the river a fountain, or the fountain a river. Nevertheless we allow that they are both one according to nature, and also one in substance; and we admit that the fountain may be conceived of as father, and that the river is what is begotten of the fountain.'*

"That should be enough to expose the fallacy in Arius's theories."

The young deacon was unconvinced. "In the case of inanimate objects with no will of their own, one thing emanates from another naturally, and so shares its substance; the source isn't free *not* to spawn the emanation. Surely Arius will argue that on a spiritual plane, whatever springs from a separate source is subordinate to its will—as the word which springs from the speaker is freely formed, and of a different nature from and subordinate to the speaker. Arius can use this volitional subordination to distinguish such physical analogies as Dionysius used."

Alexander was impressed, but not at all surprised, by his student's perceptiveness. The ability to anticipate and head off an opponent's arguments is the highest rhetorical skill of the debater, and Athanasius had that talent. "How then do you suggest we combat this virulent heresy, this denigration of Christ, if not in public debate?"

Athanasius did not hesitate. "First, you must get Arius to commit his theology to writing. Command him to submit a written exposition of his theories. That document will provide you with a fixed target, at which you may take aim with care and time for reflection, an advantage not available in the course of an unpredictable and fast-paced public debate that favors the rhetorically skilled." *Unlike you, Alexander*, the younger man thought to himself, hoping that the prelate had not taken his comment as a criticism. *If you debate him, Arius will tear you apart!*

Alexander was too focused on the solution to notice any subtle knock on his abilities. "I think commanding Arius to write out his beliefs would only give *him* that same time for care and reflection. He is far too clever and diplomatic to expose himself in anything he writes. He will couch his response in as much ambiguity as he needs to protect himself."

After hearing the passion in Arius's voice that morning, Athanasius was sure his mentor's assessment was wrong, but chose his words cautiously so as not to offend. "Perhaps that is likely; but even so, I can see no down side to asking for the written profession of faith. There is at least a chance that he will be unable to restrain himself."

"Very well," the bishop yielded after a moment's reflection. "I will make the request."

Encouraged by this acceptance of his suggestion, the capable young cleric paused briefly before offering his next one, weighing his words carefully so that Alexander would not think him too bold, nor too timid. "When Arius submits his response, shall I be permitted to review it and give you my comments?"

Alexander smiled at the deacon's ambition, and was pleased to encourage it. "I will look forward to that," he replied approvingly. "Indeed, I should like you to draft, for my review, the letter to Arius requesting an exposition of his views. Let us see how he responds. He has acknowledged Christ's pre-incarnate existence; let us see where, and indeed *if*, he attempts to draw an earlier line before which he will claim that Christ did not exist."

Athanasius was thrilled to be called to service in such a fashion, but did his best not to show it. "As you wish; I will start at once." The younger man kneeled to receive Alexander's blessing, kissed the extended hand before him, and then left quickly to return to his quarters, a spring of excitement in each step he took, relishing this opportunity to prove himself in the Archbishop's eyes.

After Athanasius departed, Alexander called to his servants for some wine, and continued to brood over the problem Arius had presented, contemplating how it might be resolved. There was something new in the Libyan's upstart Christology, something Alexander could not recall encountering in the writings of any church fathers of the past two centuries—yet something vaguely familiar as well. Could there be an element of truth in it? No, how *could* there be? How could the Wisdom of God ever *not* have been present with God, at all times? Alexander felt a brief moment of shame in even entertaining the notion that the Son might not have existed before some beginning point in time. Determined to purge himself of the thought, he went immediately to the library and spread out onto the reading table the first scroll of Origen's *De Principiis*, scanning it for the argument he dimly recalled being there—and on finding it, delighted in each line as though it were a salve, a balm against the nagging itch of uncertainty:

> "And who that is capable of entertaining reverential thoughts or feelings regarding God, can suppose or believe that God the Father ever existed, even for a moment of time, without having generated this Wisdom? For in that case he must say either that God was unable to generate Wisdom before He produced her, so that He afterwards called into being her who formerly did not exist, or that He possessed the power indeed, but— what cannot be said of God without impiety— was unwilling to use it; both of which suppositions, it is patent to all, are alike absurd and impious: for they amount to this, either that God advanced from a condition of inability to one of ability, or that, although possessed of the power, He concealed it, and delayed the generation of Wisdom. Wherefore we have always held that God is the Father of His only-begotten Son, who was born indeed of Him, and derives from Him what He is, but without any beginning, not only such as may be measured by any divisions of time, but even that which the mind alone can contemplate within itself, or behold, so to speak, with the naked powers of the understanding. And therefore we must believe that Wisdom was generated before any beginning that can be either comprehended or expressed."

Chapter 8

Sitting alone in his sparsely furnished room when the letter arrived, a simple scroll bearing Alexander's distinctive seal, Arius knew what it contained before opening it. His pulse quickened as he read it and then let it fall from his hands onto his desk. The inevitable confrontation with Alexander that he had instigated with such bravado and aplomb suddenly felt uncomfortably ominous now that it was about to escalate. But this was no time to be timid. Kneeling down, he rested his forearms on the front of the desk and pressed his brow into them, closing his eyes and praying audibly, although there was no one else to hear: *Father, you are my God, and there is no god apart from you. Impart to me a measure of your grace, that I may ever proclaim you to be One, indivisible; and against those who would seek to divide you, let me ever proclaim your only-begotten Son as the instrument of your love that divides you not.*

Arising and peering out his window at the magnificent lighthouse that dominated the Alexandrian skyline and stood like a sentinel above the busy harbor, Arius realized at once that he would be well-served by garnering as much clerical backing as possible for his response to the Archbishop. There were more than a few presbyters in Alexandria and the surrounding delta region who followed their own counsel rather than Alexander's, and Arius knew all of them well. Many had expressed agreement or at least sympathy with his theories in the past; surely, he thought, some of them could be persuaded to subscribe to his reply. That would be a start. Beyond Alexandria, particularly in Palestine and Syria where Lucian's teachings were still recalled and respected, he enjoyed the concurrence of a number of bishops and presbyters with whom he had been corresponding for many months.

Chapter 8

Now was the time to rally their support, to discover how many of them would actually take a stand in opposition to the Archbishop.

The first one he sought out was his friend Achilles, the respected director of the Catechetical School and a staunch monotheist. Together they summoned other sympathetic local presbyters and deacons: Aeithales, Carpones, Sarmates, Euzoïus, Lucius, Julius, Menas, Helladius, and Gaius, all of whom agreed to meet secretly and discuss a response to Alexander's letter. Convening on the appointed evening in the dank and dimly lit rotunda of the Catacombs tunneled into the bedrock below the eastern end of the city, they chattered nervously among themselves while waiting for the meeting to begin. Achilles called them to order and led them in prayer, then nodded at Arius. The Libyan thanked them warmly as he rose to his full impressive stature in the flickering torchlight, confidently summoning all of the oratory zeal that was his trademark:

"My dear friends, I ask you to consider for a moment the faith of the common believer. Upon being baptized into the church, he hears the Scriptures read to him and listens to his preachers expound on the pillars of our faith to which we all subscribe: that the God of Israel, creator and sovereign of the universe, sent his only Son to become incarnate of a virgin, to live as the man Jesus Christ, among us and as one of us, to teach us the way of righteousness; and though being without sin, ultimately to submit to suffering and death on the cross in atonement for our sins, as Savior and Redeemer; only to be resurrected on the third day, and thence assumed bodily into heaven, where he sits as supreme judge of the world.

"But the common believer is also instructed, and so takes on faith, that this *Son* of God actually *was* God, *is* God, equal to the Father in every respect, fully divine as well as human. He tacitly accepts that if a son of man is human, so must a Son of God be divine; and he makes no effort to square this analogy with there being many humans, but one indivisible God. He is instructed, and so believes, that although God is One and indivisible, nevertheless the Son is somehow one *with* the Father; begotten of the Father yet co-eternal with him; separate in personhood yet identical in essence; Suffering Servant yet Lord and Master; equal in rank and power yet able to declare 'The Father is greater than I'—paradoxes that he should not try to comprehend and thus does not care to comprehend.

"Moreover, he is admonished, and so accepts without question, that his salvation and redemption would have been impossible if the crucified Christ had been anything less than fully divine himself; that the shedding of blood, without which the Letter to the Hebrews assures us there is no forgiveness of sin, must of necessity have been the *divine* blood of *God incarnate* in order to wash away that sin; that no lesser solvent could be made to work, not even by an omnipotent God. But how or why that is so, how or why it was *necessary* that Jesus Christ must truly have been God himself, nothing less, in order to effectuate our salvation, is a question unanswered by Scripture and unaddressed by his preachers. At their urgings, couched in beguiling references to unfathomable mysteries, the question soon becomes unimportant to him. 'Let the catechumens debate such philosophical niceties,' they tell him if he should be so impious as to inquire further, 'for you are saved by grace, not by theology. It is enough that the Son of God died on the cross to atone for your sins, and as all agree on that key point, the true nature of that Son who died for those sins need not be limned.' They even quote to him from the Psalm, '*I do not occupy myself with things too great and too marvelous for me.*'

"My dear colleagues, it is for the sake of such common believers that I call upon you now. Without instruction or understanding, how easily they are led into error by those who claim true knowledge of the nature of God and His Christ! How quickly they are lured away from using their own God-given reason, distracted by flourishes of symbolism and allegory, by pious-sounding references to mystical concepts! It is no wonder that Marcion, Valentinus, Basilides, Manichæus, Sabellius and many others have found them to be such easy prey for all manner of heresies; for their rationality has been dulled by their own church! The result is plain: we see everywhere dissensions, schisms, factions, utter lack of consensus on doctrinal matters. From the beginning the holy church has been persecuted from without; but she persecutes *herself* from within!

"Here is our opportunity to strike a blow for rationality, to free the mind of the common believer from the impediments to understanding that have for so long been placed as obstacles in its way! Here is our chance to rescue the message of Scripture from the base contamination of Greek sophistry, to restore the purity of God's word, enjoined on Israel in the command to be separate from other nations and stressed by Paul in his warning to the Colossians not to be held captive by philosophy and empty deceit! Shall we not seize this moment? Shall we not rise as one and combine our voices so that Alexander, and all Alexandrians, and indeed all believers throughout the world can hear us? Shall we not proclaim the truth that God is *One*, and resist those who would make Him into *two*, God

Chapter 8

the Father and God the Son? For if two, why not three? Or *more*? Where will this needless multiplication of deities end, or where will this needless division of the one deity end, if the line is not drawn where God himself has drawn it? My brothers, who among you is ready to defend the *Shema*? Declare with me now!"

The passion stirring in the subterranean hall was palpable. Arius had found his first allies.

Chapter 9

"Read it to me again," Alexander demanded, closing his eyes in concentration as he leaned back against the sill of his chamber window, oblivious to the scouring rain falling outside and the rolls of punctuating thunder. "Slowly." Athanasius inhaled deeply and began anew:

"*To Our Blessed Pope and Bishop, Alexander, the Presbyters and Deacons send health in the Lord. Our faith from our forefathers, which also we have learned from thee, Blessed Pope, is this:—We acknowledge One God, alone Ingenerate, alone Everlasting, alone Unbegun, alone True, alone having Immortality, alone Wise, alone Good, alone Sovereign; Judge, Governor, and Providence of all, unalterable and unchangeable, just and good, God of Law and Prophets and New Testament; who begat an Only-begotten Son before eternal times, through whom He has made both the ages and the universe; and begat Him, not in semblance, but in truth; and that He made Him subsist at His own will, unalterable and unchangeable; perfect creature of God, but not as one of the creatures; offspring, but not as one of things begotten; nor as Valentinus pronounced that the offspring of the Father was an issue; nor as Manichæus taught that the offspring was a portion of the Father, one in essence; or as Sabellius, dividing the Monad, speaks of a Son-and-Father; nor as Hieracas, of one torch from another, or as a lamp divided into two; nor that He who was before, was afterwards generated or new-created into a Son, as thou too thyself, Blessed Pope, in the midst of the Church and in session hast often condemned; but, as we say, at the will of God, created before times and before ages, and gaining life and being from the Father, who gave subsistence to His glories together with Him. For the Father did not, in giving to Him* the inheritance of all things, deprive Himself of what He has ingenerately in Himself; for He is the Fountain of all things.

"'Thus there are Three Subsistences. And God, being the cause of all things, is Unbegun and altogether Sole, but the Son being begotten apart from time by the Father, and being created and founded before ages, was not before His generation, but being begotten apart from time before all things, alone was made to subsist by the Father. For He is not eternal or co-eternal or co-unoriginate with the Father, nor has He His being together with the Father, as some speak of relations, introducing two ingenerate beginnings, but God is before all things as being Monad and Beginning of all.

"'Wherefore also He is before the Son; as we have learned also from thy preaching in the midst of the Church. So far then as from God He has being, and glories and life, and all things are delivered unto Him, in such sense is God His origin. For He is above Him, as being His God and before Him. But if the terms 'from Him,' and 'from the womb,' and 'I came forth from the Father, and I am come,' be understood by some to mean as if a part of Him, one in essence or as an issue, then the Father is according to them compounded and divisible and alterable and material, and, as far as their belief goes, has the circumstances of a body, Who is the Incorporeal God.' And it is signed by those I mentioned, Arius's name first."

Alexander frowned when the deacon had finished, and began to pace around the room nervously, his fingers scratching at his scalp through his thin white hair. "Do you see how this devious priest constructs his conclusions so carefully from seemingly innocuous premises? He acknowledges three hypostases, but sets them in a hierarchy of dependence that excludes any full sharing of divinity. His sole measure of divinity is the quality of being 'ingenerate,' self-existent. Since the Father alone is ingenerate, no other being who has been generated or begotten—the Son included—can be fully divine, nor be 'one in essence' with the Father. Even being 'created before times and before ages' and 'begotten apart from time before all things' ultimately makes no difference in Arius's theology; the Son cannot share fully in the essence of the Father simply because, not being ingenerate, there was a time when the Son 'was not.'"

"I see in this a shadow of Origen's Commentary on John's gospel," Athanasius noted. "Origen similarly wrote 'We consider, therefore, that there are three hypostases, the Father and the Son and the Holy Spirit; and at the same time we believe nothing to be uncreated but the Father.' Perhaps Arius is planning to take refuge in Origen here."

Heresy

"Indeed. And we must flush him out from that cover. But how?"

Athanasius was quick to respond. "Arius mentions nothing about Origen's doctrine of eternal generation; he simply equates 'generated' and 'begotten' with 'created,' without further discussion. Perhaps there is an avenue of attack for us here."

"What is the difference, Athanasius? In the end, are they not the same?"

"Not at all. 'Son' and 'creature' are incompatible notions. What is made or created is fashioned by a craftsman, not sired by a father. The distinction we must hold to is that between being immediately brought forth out of the generator's substance, and being created out of nothing. Just as heat is generated by fire, but not created by fire. If the fire always existed, so did the heat—uncreated, though begotten of and generated by the fire. Grant that the one be uncreated, it follows that the other is uncreated as well. One does not exist without the other, and there was never a time when the fire was, but the heat was not."

Alexander was dubious. "Did you not caution me earlier to be wary of analogies to the physical world and its objects, which lack a will of their own? All material things have intrinsic qualities or properties which can be described; as, for example, fire has the property of heat. We must be careful not to portray the Son as a mere quality or property of the Father, as the Sabellians do, impersonal and without a separate hypostasis. For unlike the fire which generates the heat, the Father *willed* that the Son proceed from him. Divine will is the very font of creation; as Origen wrote: '*the will of the Father ought alone to be sufficient for the existence of that which He wishes to exist. . . And thus also the existence of the Son is generated by Him. For this point must above all others be maintained by those who allow nothing to be unbegotten, i.e., unborn, save God the Father only.*' Unless we are to reject Origen altogether, our challenge will be to respond to Arius's claim that whatever is brought about by the will of God—even the Son, whose generation Arius insists was an act of the Father's will—must therefore have been created out of nothing."

"And here is where the distinction between *created* by God's will and simply *begotten* must be maintained," Athanasius offered in reply. "We must not confuse the two concepts as Arius does, even if we grant that both result from the will of God. Not every expression of God's will entails creation out of nothing. A fire ignited by a lightning bolt is surely not created out of nothing simply because the bolt was sent by God's will. Similarly may the

Son issue forth by the Father's will without entailing the conclusion that the Son was created out of nothing."

The Archbishop remained skeptical. "Examples of God's will that merely transform one thing into another rather than create it out of nothing prove only the *possibility* of uncreative divine will; they do not prove that it is true of the Son. Nor would we want it to; the Son is not in any sense a transformation of the Father. We will need something more than physical analogies such as lightning to fire, or fire to heat, if we are to persuade Arius's followers of his errors. We must find a way to explain the notion that the Son was generated by the Father's will without entailing the subordination that Arius asserts."

Athanasius sighed heavily. "If so, that is our misfortune. We have only our human experience to draw upon in fashioning our explanations. To analogize divine will to human will, implying a desire for something not yet present, surely misdescribes it—for the divine will, like eternity itself, is ineffable. Nothing in our human experience equips us to understand and explain such matters. I recall the words of Origen's disciple Gregory Thaumaturgus, Bishop of Neo-Caesarea: *'Besides, the generation of the Son by the Father is incomprehensible and ineffable; and because it is spiritual, its investigation becomes impracticable: for a spiritual object can neither be understood nor traced by a corporeal object, for that is far removed from human nature.'* I fear that we may arrive at that point before long."

Alexander's face reddened with frustration as he turned toward the window, watching the relentless rain pelt the street below. He raised his voice louder, his tone decisive. "Then we will quash this upstart dissension by the force of ecclesiastical authority," he resolved. "God forbid that I should stand idly by while so central a dogma as the divinity of our Lord Jesus Christ, handed down by tradition and sealed by the blood of martyrs, is assaulted by these misguided clerics! We will test their resolve by condemning this apostasy, and we shall see how many of them back down. Go now and draft a statement of condemnation at once, Athanasius. I will summon a council of all the clergy here in the city and from throughout Egypt, even from Libya—and if they do as I expect, the sheer number of signatures affixed to that statement will make Arius gasp at how much opposition there is to his errant ideas. His partisans will not dare to go out onto a limb that extends so far from the trunk; they must be shown just how far out of the mainstream they have ventured, before they dare to venture further and fall

Heresy

to their doom. As for Arius himself, I will strip him of his congregation and excommunicate him. This heresy ends *now*!"

Chapter 10

Through the thick early morning fog that rolled in from the sea and swallowed the shoreline, an embittered Arius walked along the Baucalis waterfront as he waited for his ship to begin boarding, wondering when he would next have the opportunity to stroll these familiar streets. Events had certainly not turned out as expected. Instead of the open debate he had hoped to lure Alexander into, Arius had provoked him to convene a synod of Egyptian and Libyan bishops and presbyters who were only too willing to bow to the Archbishop's authority and condemn Arius's teachings. *A flock of cowardly sheep, nothing more*, he muttered to himself. Sadly, the courage to stand up to the prelate was in short supply. And now, here he was, excommunicated and banished—again!

He began to question himself. Why hadn't he seen this coming? How could he have so badly misjudged Alexander's power and influence over the local clergy, including many whom he had counted among his followers? Was he blinded by his own pride, his own ambition? The shrill calls of the seabirds along the shore seemed to mock him, laughing at his foolishness. He could not blame them.

The prospect of foregoing the amicable society of the Alexandrian priests and deacons who had sympathized with him, and especially the thought of leaving his beloved congregation behind, drove Arius to tears, and then to anger. But he knew that resistance was pointless. At first he had wondered whether the devotees of his pastorate in Baucalis would challenge Alexander's edict and insist that he stay on to minister to them; and indeed, there was some initial sentiment for precisely that. In the end, fearful of exposing his congregants to similar excommunication, Arius did not press the issue. The Archbishop commanded far too much authority, and there was no point embroiling his followers in a dispute that could not end well for them.

Still, Arius was steadfast in his resolve to turn a negative into a positive, confident that the truth could not be stifled merely by episcopal denunciation, even from so respected a bishopric as Alexander's. No doubt the prelate would try to convince others outside of his See to censure Arius's teachings as well; but the sway that Alexander held over free-thinking bishops and presbyters elsewhere was uncertain. A number of them had already expressed some sympathy with Arius's views. There was a whole world waiting out there, filled with potential supporters. If Alexandria was no longer a hospitable base for spreading his message, so be it; Palestine would do nicely. Hadn't Origen himself, upon falling out of favor with his bishop Demetrius, fled from Alexandria to Caesarea to continue his writing and open a new school of theology? *Yes*, Arius thought, a perfect precedent to follow. He had many friends and sympathizers in Caesarea, including its respected bishop Eusebius, who was called "Pamphilus" after his teacher, the former head of Caesarea's impressive theological library. Perhaps that library could be a resource for Arius to continue his studies, which now had but a single focus. Perhaps Eusebius would take up his cause.

Yet it was another bishop named Eusebius, not of Caesarea but of Nicomedia, that Arius was counting on for the most support. Many years earlier the two had studied together in Antioch under Lucian, and they had kept in regular contact over the years. Nicomedia was the capital city of the eastern Roman Empire, the seat of co-emperor Licinius, and the church there had great influence, rivaling that of Alexandria. If Eusebius of Nicomedia could be counted on as a patron to defend the doctrine Arius taught, not even Alexander would be able to curtail its reception beyond Egypt.

Boarding his ship, Arius caught sight of the great Lighthouse as the shroud of fog began to thin above the dark water of the harbor. This time he saw it as an agent for truth—Alexandria illuminating the world, he thought, not as a beacon to guide others to itself, but a light to remove the darkness surrounding them right where they stood, revealing the truth that had been obscured by the vanity of ignorant men. Out of Egypt had God called his Son, and out of Egypt would come the clarifier of the Son's true nature. This banishment, Arius thought, was but a temporary setback; he remained determined to expose the error to which his opponents clung so tenaciously. For them, the Son they worshipped *must* share a single divine substance with the Father, lest they be accused of worshipping a mere creature, which they view as idolatry, or of acknowledging two Gods, which is likewise idolatry—or, worse still, of something approaching Sabellianism, the teaching that Christ is not really distinct from the Father at all, but rather the Father himself in the guise of human flesh, a fictitious son, a mere aspect of the one God. And to save themselves from this perceived dilemma and adopt the position they felt compelled to reach, they were willing to sacrifice all logic.

How, he wondered, could any right thinking person fail to see that the Alexandrian position was logically inconsistent? All one needed to do was lay out their tenets side by side, and the contradiction became stark: they insisted (1) there is one God; (2) the Father is God; (3) the Father is not the Son; yet (4) the Son is fully God. Simple logic demanded that all four propositions cannot be simultaneously held; the fourth *cannot* be true if the first three are. The more Arius considered the matter, the more incredulous he became. Why won't they let it go? Why must they cling to irrationality? At least Sabellius, for all his faults, had a logically consistent theory: (1) there is one God; (2) the Father is God; (3) the Son is God; therefore (4) *the Father is the Son*. Heresy this may be; but not absurdity!

As Arius saw it, the Alexandrians compounded their error by divorcing their theology from its Jewish roots. The *Shema*, he was convinced, is more than a statement about quantity; it is also a declaration of quality, of *essential* oneness, of indivisibility. Couldn't they see that for any other being to share in the substance of the Father would render the Father divisible, and *not* unique and transcendent? What other conclusion could there be except that the unique and indivisible God did not and *could* not communicate his own being, *could* not impart his own absolute oneness and unique self-subsistence, to any other being —for to share in it is necessarily to destroy it—and thus that any other being, including the Son, must of necessity have been created from *non*-being? Yes, Arius thought to himself, he would show Christians everywhere a way out of their logical dilemma *without* joining the Sabellians and denying any real distinction between Father and Son. All he needed was their attention.

He was about to get it. Arius had correctly gauged Alexander's next move—a letter writing campaign designed to poison any well that Arius's dissident movement might turn to for refreshment. Even as Arius was preparing to leave the city, dozens of letters were being dispatched to bishops throughout Europe and Asia, warning them of Arius and his heretical allies.

But Alexander's efforts to prevent a local apostasy from becoming a worldwide one would soon spark the very thing he sought to avoid. By calling the schism to the attention of bishops everywhere, his letters would provide a measure of familiarity to later overtures by Arius and his supporters, overtures that they might otherwise simply ignore as the rumblings of some insignificant movement of minor clerics. Once their interest was piqued, their minds could be swayed; and the more that were swayed, the more the movement would gain momentum. Soon, he hoped, Alexander would find himself opposing an ever growing number of bishops throughout the Empire. Arius smiled at the notion. "Yes, my dear Alexander," he reckoned to himself, "I do believe that in the end, you may have done me a service!"

As the sun burned off the remaining wisps of fog, a sudden gust of wind stiffened the sails with a loud crack, thrusting the ship forward into the Mediterranean. Arius looked behind at the receding harbor and caught sight of the church building that had served as his preaching post for the past decade, a spiritual home for hundreds of his faithful congregants. Had he fully opened their eyes to the truth? Had he rooted them sufficiently to withstand the attacks on his teaching that would surely be mounted by his replacement? How many would stay the course during his absence? Only time would tell. The matter was out of his hands now, and into God's. It was time to sow other seeds elsewhere.

With a renewed sense of purpose Arius turned toward the bow of the ship and gazed ahead across the shimmering sea.

Chapter 11

Ever since I first saw it as a child, I have had a loathing of the eastern Egyptian desert, the dry and hilly region that lies between the Nile and the Red Sea. The farther south one ventures up the great river, the narrower becomes the sustenance afforded by its verdant valley, and the more leaving it behind to enter the desert feels like crossing the very border of life into the realm of death. The desert drinks the same light as the city, from the same sun, but extracts its bitterness rather than its sweetness. This is a region fit for demons, not men. Indeed, where else could demons find a home, now that they have been driven from the cities and villages by the triumph of Christ's church? Anyone who ventures to live in this barren land must be prepared to wrestle with them.

Such a man is blessed Anthony, the famed hermit whose counsel I now go to seek. Here at the edge of the eastern desert, in the ruins of the long-abandoned Roman fort at Mount Pispir where he first set up his hermitage and spent twenty solitary years striving with demons, I have come to speak with him. This spot, some fifty miles south of Memphis, is now his "Outer Mountain," where dozens of his followers, drawn by his reputation and example, have set up their own ascetic community, living in sparse cells hewn into the rock and devoting themselves to prayer and the contemplative life. Anthony himself has long since moved on, living alone in his "Inner Mountain" two days' journey by caravan to the east, farther into the desert. It is said that he returns to the Outer Mountain only infrequently, several times a year, to advise and encourage his disciples. Rarely does he suffer visits from the many outsiders who make pilgrimages to this place, motivated by the hope of miraculous healings or the desire for hidden wisdom. To those he deigns to receive he devotes but little time; and only slightly more is lavished on prospective disciples seeking to adopt the monastic discipline he established.

A hermit's lifestyle holds no appeal to me. While I cannot disparage the choices made by others, I find that the service of Christ and his church obliges me to minister *to* the world, not retreat from it. Didn't Jesus concern himself intimately in the lives of the common folk he met, always returning to minister to them after he had gone off for a while to pray alone? Nevertheless, I have little doubt that Anthony has been called to be a servant of Christ as well, although in a different way. Here in the desert, free of mundane distractions, the knowledge he has gained of God has been direct, in heavenly divinations and visions garnered through the faith he practices in its purest form, trusting completely in the words preached to him long ago: "*Therefore do not worry, saying, 'What will we eat?' or 'What will we drink?' or 'What will we wear?.' For it is the Gentiles who strive for all these things; and indeed your heavenly Father knows that you need all these things. But strive first for the kingdom of God and his righteousness, and all these things will be given to you as well . . .*" And the kingdom of God that he thus sought, he surely found. Within himself. Precisely where Christ said it could be found.

The sure knowledge of Christ's true nature that I hope to receive from this mystic saint—if he will meet with me—arises from revelation, although not the kind found in the sacred writings. I have strained mightily to distill that knowledge from Scripture, each time extracting only an inconclusive dross. The Hebrew writings yield only tantalizingly ambiguous hints. Paul's epistles address the issue equivocally. The gospels are mostly silent on the matter, and where they are not, their treatment of it is indirect. John's comes closest to a direct answer, but in the end even his gospel is fraught with ambiguities: the same incarnate Word who is portrayed as God in the opening verses is nevertheless described as announcing the *Father's* kingdom, the one by whom he was sent, the one whose work he is doing, the one whom he proclaims as "greater than I." What I have been taught and believe about the nature of the Son finds only limited corroboration in the written word. I am eager to confirm my beliefs—eager enough to seek confirmation from one who, perhaps, communicates more directly with God than I have ever been able to manage.

Anthony is indeed at the Outer Mountain when I arrive. Standing like sentinels in the blazing hot sun, his gatekeepers swat at the merciless sand

Chapter 11

flies and eye me warily, until I let it be known that I am Alexander's personal secretary. They presume that I have come on his behalf, and I let them presume. They attend to my camel, and the meeting is hastily arranged.

The holy monk greets me in an exposed recess of the old fort, open on two sides and sheltered under the cover of a canvas, with two small overturned buckets that serve as chairs. We sit. I am both surprised and gratified to see that Anthony, now in his late sixties, is still in good health, appearing little worse for the wear of what has surely been a life of physical hardship, evidenced only by the deep furrows in his well-tanned face. Great men impress with command in their bearing and confidence in their tone; but it is otherwise with Anthony. His serene countenance, offset by his penetrating eyes, puts me in awe. He asks if I wish to pray with him, and without waiting for an answer leads us in prayer. Then he offers me some water, although taking none himself, and I gratefully accept. I inquire politely about his years in the desert, but he tells me little of substance, steering the conversation instead toward my concerns. I tell him of Arius. Yes, he says, he has heard. I question him about the eternal sonship of God's only-begotten, and whether he believes that Father and Son share fully the same uniquely divine essence. He leans forward, resting his elbows on his knees and tenting his fingertips, touching them to his chin as he studies me intently. After a measured silence, he asks me if I have considered what might be impairing my own certainty on the subject. The lack of explicit confirmation in Scripture, I respond. He seems dubious, and tells me it is folly to expect from Scripture an unequivocal answer to every theological question. I ask where, then, they are to be found. He peers directly into my eyes and gently responds: "Why, within your own heart, of course. God reveals himself to those who truly seek him; but we must do so in the proper spirit."

I ask him whether he himself has ever pondered the question of the Son's true nature and relation to the Father, or sought its answer from God. He replies that he has not, that the solitude of the desert has taught him to temper and curb intellectual curiosity about the nature of God, which is beyond the capacity of human reason to grasp on its own but well within God's capacity to implant through faith. He promptly assures me he will nevertheless pray that I find the answers I seek. Deflecting the obvious next question, he rises from his seat, thanks me for making the arduous journey, and exhorts me to express his good wishes to the Archbishop. The audience is at an end. It is evident that Anthony does not want to be asked to intercede further.

As I turn to leave, I suddenly understand why. This is *my* inquiry, not his, and for that reason he *cannot* obtain an answer for me. God is revealed to those who *truly* seek him, and Anthony would not be true in seeking a dialogue with God to satisfy another's curiosity.

Do *I* truly seek him? If anything, my coming here suggests that I do not; I suddenly see this entire excursion for what it was, an ill-conceived effort to take a short cut where square corners must be humbly turned. Setting out on this journey in the hope of receiving one lesson, I am returning home with another—but perhaps, one of greater value. It is often difficult to see ourselves as we truly are, without illusion. After just a brief time with Anthony, my self-imposed view of myself as both devout and learned has been stripped bare. I have been engaging the question of God's triune nature not as it is, but as *I* am, through *my* perspectives, as though it were an intellectual exercise, a puzzle to be solved by painstakingly piecing together tantalizing Scriptural clues. Clearly I still have much to learn.

A dry wind whirls dancing circles of sand around my feet as I mount my camel. I shield my eyes from the searing sun and goad the beast down toward the ribbon of river in the distance, where my boat is waiting. He knows the route to take. I am the one struggling for direction. Has my approach really been wrongheaded all along? Could it be that knowledge of Christ's true nature lies not in what the Scriptures report that Christ said of himself, nor in what the prophets and apostles said of him, but in the divine activity of redemption to which their statements attest, working itself out in the faith of the believer?

Chapter 12

As bishop of the powerful See of Nicomedia, Eusebius was accustomed to receiving correspondence from other Christian prelates and clergy throughout the empire. Some letters bore petty complaints; others were simply greetings; still others were from colleagues sharing information and seeking Eusebius' opinion on various religious matters; but many sought political advice. Tensions between Constantine and Licinius, co-rulers of the Roman Empire, had been mounting for years, to the point where military conflict now seemed inevitable. Because Licinius maintained his imperial capital in Nicomedia and many in his court were Christians whom Eusebius had befriended and counseled, the bishop was widely viewed as having valuable insight—especially into Licinius' increasing hostility toward Christians, whom he perceived as uncomfortably friendly toward Constantine.

On this day, however, the letter that particularly caught Eusebius' attention was from an old friend:

> *"To his very dear lord, the man of God, the faithful and orthodox Eusebius, Arius, unjustly persecuted by Alexander the Pope, on account of that all conquering truth of which you also are a champion, send greeting in the Lord.*
>
> *"Ammonius, my father, being about to depart for Nicomedia, I considered myself bound to salute you by him, and withal to inform that natural affection which you bear towards the brethren for the sake of God and His Christ, that the bishop greatly wastes and persecutes us, and leaves no stone unturned against us. He has driven us out of the city as atheists, because we do not concur in what he publicly preaches, namely, God always, the Son always; as the Father*

Heresy

so the Son; the Son co-exists unbegotten with the God; He is everlasting; neither by thought nor by any interval does God precede the Son; always God, always Son; he is begotten of the unbegotten; the Son is of God Himself. Eusebius, your brother bishop of Caesarea, Theodotus, Paulinus, Athanasius, Gregorius, Aetius, and all the bishops of the East, have been condemned because they say that God had an existence prior to that of his Son; except Philogonius, Hellanicus, and Macarius, who are unlearned men, and who have embraced heretical opinions. Some of them say that the Son is an eructation, others that He is a production, others the He is also unbegotten.

"These are impieties to which we cannot listen, even though heretics threaten us with a thousand deaths. But we say and believe, and have taught, and do teach, that the Son is not unbegotten; and that He does not derive his subsistence from any matter; but that by His own will and counsel He has subsisted before time, and before ages, as perfect God, only begotten and unchangeable, and that before He was begotten, or created, or purposed, or established, He was not. For He was not unbegotten. We are persecuted, because we say that the Son has a beginning, but that God is without beginning.

"This is the cause of our persecution, and likewise, because we say that He is of the non-existent. And this we say, because He is neither part of God, nor of any essential being. For this are we persecuted; the rest you know. I bid thee farewell in the Lord, remembering our afflictions, my fellow-Lucianist, and true Eusebius."

Eusebius could not suppress a slight smile as he finished reading. For some time now he had been following the controversy closely in correspondence with a number of bishops, and had already begun to lend his own prestige to Arius's side of it, but it was refreshing to receive a concise statement like this from the instigator himself. Clearly the passion that Arius had displayed in his youth still flamed, no less than his skill in writing. He had managed to capture the imaginations of Christians far beyond Alexandria. This was far bigger than Arius now. It was a movement. And Eusebius resolved to throw his full support behind it.

Calling his secretary to his spacious chambers, Eusebius promptly dictated a reply to Arius, urging him to hold fast to the truth: "Since you think properly, pray that everyone will think that way. For it is clear to all that the thing which is made did not exist before it came into being; but rather what came into being has a beginning to its existence."

That the Son had a beginning to *its* existence was, Eusebius knew, not a new concept originated by his Libyan friend. Even the Latin apologist

Chapter 12

Tertullian, normally a champion of trinitarian thought, had made such a suggestion a century earlier in his polemic text *Against Hermogenes*:

> "Because God is in like manner a Father, and He is also a Judge; but He has not always been Father and Judge, merely on the ground of His having always been God. For He could not have been the Father previous to the Son, nor a Judge previous to sin. There was, however, a time when neither sin existed with Him, nor the Son; the former of which was to constitute the Lord a Judge, and the latter a Father."

Still, Eusebius knew that other respected church fathers held a different view. This controversy would not be resolved by mustering competing texts and counting which camp had the most favoring its side. Opinions would be swayed as much by the power of logic as by the weight of scholarly authority. But for any argument to be logically persuasive to the majority of church leaders, Eusebius realized that above all else, it would need to accommodate and explain the prologue to the fourth gospel. And here, he planned to offer Arius some help.

Through all his studies over the years, Eusebius had developed a fascination with John's use of the *Logos* concept to describe the Son of God, a concept that appeared nowhere elsewhere in Scripture. To understand John's association properly, discovering its true antecedents was key, and Eusebius was convinced that he had. Eusebius recognized a simple ambiguity in John's gospel: that the *Logos* existed "in the beginning" left unanswered the question, "beginning" of *what*? Surely not the beginning of *God*, for God has no beginning. The Book of Genesis opened with the same phrase, and clearly referred to the beginning of *creation*. Eusebius was convinced that John must have intended the same meaning for his own use of the phrase. After all, John likewise portrayed the *Logos* as the creative power of God, the agent through which creation was achieved: "All things came into being through him, and without him not one thing came into being." John was simply being true to Genesis, which declared that the heavens and the earth were created by God's word; God *said* "Let there be light," and there was light; and so on. For John, then, the *Logos* was God's creative expression, and the phrase "in the beginning" meant "at the point of creation." Therefore, Eusebius reasoned, when John wrote that "the Word was God," he could be understood as describing the *creative power* of God—in the manner expounded by Philo of Alexandria.

The eminent Jewish theologian Philo, Eusebius thought, had an advantageous perspective on the nature of the *Logos* precisely because he was a Jew, because he was *not* Christian, and thus free of the overlay of the incarnate Son, the person of Jesus Christ, that subtly cluttered most Christians' attempts to conceptualize the *Logos*. Decades before John wrote his gospel, Philo had likewise taught that the *Logos* was the creative agent of God. Following Greek philosophical distinctions between types of causes, Philo held that God is the *efficient* cause, *by whom* the cosmos was made, while the *Logos* was the *instrumental* cause, *by means of which* the cosmos was made. This subtle distinction was recognized even by Paul, his contemporary, who wrote to the Corinthians of "one God, the Father, from whom are all things and for whom we exist, and one Lord, Jesus Christ, through whom are all things and through whom we exist." For Philo as for Paul, the creative *Logos* was also the "image" of God referenced in Genesis' telling phrase, "Let us make mankind in our image." Philo wrote in his famous *Questions and Answers on Genesis*:

> *"Why is it that he speaks as if of some other god, saying that he made man after the image of God, and not that he made him after his own image? Very appropriately and without any falsehood was this oracular sentence uttered by God, for no mortal thing could have been formed on the similitude of the supreme Father of the universe, but only after the pattern of the* **second deity***, who is the Word of the supreme Being."*

Yet, for Philo, as for Origen, calling the creative *Logos* a "second deity" entailed no retreat from monotheism, because this second principle remained subordinate to the first. As Philo wrote in his *Questions and Answers on Exodus*:

> *"In the first place (there is) He Who is elder than the one and the monad and the beginning. Then (comes) the Logos of the Existent One, the truly seminal substance of existing things. And from the divine Logos, as from a spring, there divide and break forth two powers. One is the creative (power), through which the Artificer placed and ordered all things; this is named 'God.' And (the other is) the royal (power), since through it the Creator rules over created things; this is called 'Lord.'"*

In all of this, Eusebius saw a useful explanation of the declaration of identity in John's opening verse, one that avoided characterizing the *Logos* as the God of transcendence by designating it as the God of creation. Thus could Philo confidently declare, in his discourse on *Allegorical Interpretation*, that

Chapter 12

"the Word of God is over all the world, and is the most ancient, and the most universal of all the things that are *created*."

So could Arius. Yes, Eusebius thought to himself, it all made perfect sense. Understood in the right context, John's prologue presented no obstacle to the Arian view of the *Logos* as both creative and created, both exalted and subordinate. The framework for such a theology was already in place. Philo of Alexandria had already done the heavy lifting.

But just as the Genesis story recounted that darkness covered the formless void *before* God created light—the same light shining in the darkness that John's opening chapter associates with the *Logos*—there was a time when the created universe itself did not exist. So too, Eusebius thought, must there have been a time when the creative *Logos* did not exist, for creation would instantaneously follow from the *Logos*' existence; it made no sense to think of the *Logos* in the abstract, merely potential, dormant. An unspoken word is no Word at all. What better proof that the *Logos* was itself not eternal? In God, the Word may have been dormant and potential. But not in itself. Not as a separate hypostasis.

The bishop smiled as he called his secretary back in to his chambers and began dictating again.

Chapter 13

When word of Eusebius' support for Arius reached Alexander, he sent for Athanasius immediately. The young deacon found him strolling in his expansive walled garden, with the chirping of birds and the fragrant smell of fig trees, pomegranates and lemons filling the summer air. Despite the idyllic setting, Athanasius could see at once that the bishop was distressed. "It seems that we have a new and more powerful enemy," he told his protégé, handing him the letter that had just arrived from Nicomedia. Alexander did not wait for Athanasius to finish reading it, and continued to pace as he spoke, the deacon trailing behind as he read the missive and listened to the bishop at the same time. "This Eusebius is an ambitious, power-hungry fool, another misguided disciple of Lucian of Antioch like the heretic he means to support. It is time to marshal the forces of truth against him. We must oppose him in the strongest terms—and without delay."

"How may I be of service, my lord?" the youth asked excitedly.

"I plan to assemble the leaders of the church here in Egypt to join in our condemnation of this heresy, in an encyclical that will be sent to bishops throughout the world! I am relying on you, my good Athanasius, to draft that encyclical. You know my mind on this. Go now, and use all your learning, all your skills, praying to God for guidance."

Prayer was exactly what Athanasius had in mind when he left Alexander's residence. He knew well what was at stake. This was no mean philosophical dispute between Alexandrian and Antiochene schools, no setting off of Platonic and Stoic systems of thought against each other. This was a struggle for the very soul of Christianity. He threw himself into the task

Chapter 13

with all the energy he could summon, praying that God would guide his hand.

Within a day Athanasius had prepared what he was certain was an inspired document, and proudly brought it to Alexander for the patriarch's review. Alexander directed him to read it aloud at once. The younger man cleared his throat and began:

"*To our beloved and most reverend fellow-ministers of the Catholic Church in every place, Alexander sends greeting in the Lord:*

"*Since the body of the Catholic Church is one, and it is commanded in Holy Scripture that we should keep the bond of unanimity and peace, it follows that we should write and signify to one another the things which are done by each of us; that whether one member suffer or rejoice we may all either suffer or rejoice with one another. In our diocese, then, not so long ago, there have gone forth lawless men, and adversaries of Christ, teaching men to apostatize; which thing, with good right, one might suspect and call the precursor of Antichrist. I indeed wished to cover the matter up in silence, that so perhaps the evil might spend itself in the leaders of the heresy alone, and that it might not spread to other places and defile the ears of any of the more simple-minded. But since Eusebius, the present bishop of Nicomedia, is set over these apostates, and has undertaken to write everywhere, commending them, it became necessary for me no longer to remain silent, but to announce to you all, that you may know both those who have become apostates, and also the wretched words of their heresy; and if Eusebius write, not to give heed to him.*

"*Now the apostates from the Church are these: Arius, Achilles, Aithales, Carpones, the other Arius, Sarmates, who were formerly priests; Euzoius, Lucius, Julius, Menas, Helladius, and Gaius, formerly deacons; and with them Secundus and Theonas, who were once called bishops. And the words invented by them, and spoken contrary to the mind of Scripture, are as follows:—*

> '*God was not always the Father; but there was a time when God was not the Father. The Word of God was not always, but was made 'from things that are not;' for He who is God fashioned the non-existing from the non-existing; wherefore there was a time when He was not. For the Son is a thing created, and a thing made: nor is He like to the Father in substance; nor is He the true and natural Word of the Father; nor is He His true Wisdom; but He is one of the things fashioned and made. And He is called, by a misapplication of the terms, the Word and Wisdom, since He is Himself made by the proper Word of God, and by that wisdom which is in God, in which,*

Heresy

as God made all other things, so also did He make Him. Wherefore, He is by His very nature changeable and mutable, equally with other rational beings. The Word, too, is alien and separate from the substance of God. The Father also is ineffable to the Son; for neither does the Word perfectly and accurately know the Father, neither can He perfectly see Him. For neither does the Son indeed know His own substance as it is. Since He for our sakes was made, that by Him as by an instrument God might create us; nor would He have existed had not God wished to make us. Someone asked of them whether the Son of God could change even as the devil changed; and they feared not to answer that He can; for since He was made and created, He is of mutable nature.'

"Since those about Arius speak these things and shamelessly maintain them, we, coming together with the Bishops of Egypt and the Libyas, nearly a hundred in number, have anathematized them, together with their followers. For who ever heard such things? or who, now hearing them, is not astonished, and does not stop his ears that the pollution of these words should not touch them? Who that hears John saying, 'In the beginning was the Word,' does not condemn those who say there was a time when He was not? Who that hears these words of the Gospel, 'the only-begotten Son;' and, 'by Him were all things made,' will not hate those who declare He is one of the things made? For how can He be one of the things made by Him? or how shall He be the only-begotten who, as they say, is reckoned with all the rest, if indeed He is a thing made and created? And how can He be made of things which are not, when the Father says, "My heart belched forth a good Word;" and, "From the womb, before the morning have I begotten Thee?" Or how is He unlike to the substance of the Father, who is the perfect image and brightness of the Father, and who says, 'He that hath seen Me hath seen the Father?' And how, if the Son is the Word or Wisdom and Reason of God, was there a time when He was not? It is all one as if they said, that there was a time when God was without reason and wisdom. How, also, can He be changeable and mutable, who says indeed by Himself: 'I am in the Father, and the Father in Me,' and, 'I and My Father are one;' and by the prophet, 'I am the Lord, I change not?'

"Since, therefore, our Lord and Savior Jesus Christ has thus Himself exhorted us, and by His apostle hath signified such things to us; we, who have heard their impiety with our own ears, have consistently anathematized such men, as I have already said, and have declared them to be aliens from the Catholic Church and faith, and we have made known the thing, beloved and most honored fellow-ministers, to your piety, that you should not receive any *of them, should they venture rashly to come unto you, and that you should not trust Eusebius or anyone else who writes concerning them. For it becomes us as Christians to turn with aversion from all who speak or think against Christ, as the adversaries of God and the destroyers of souls, and 'not even to wish them Godspeed, lest at any time we become partakers of their evil deeds,' as the blessed John enjoins. Salute the brethren who are with you. Those who are with me salute you."*

When he had finished, Athanasius glanced anxiously at Alexander for the latter's approval. Had he gone too far? Was his tone too vitriolic? He needn't have worried. 'My son," the Archbishop nodded with a broad smile, "I would not change a single word! Let us call for the copyists at once; I want a hundred letters ready for signatures when our synod meets!"

Chapter 14

Throughout the Eastern Mediterranean, Alexander's excoriating letters quickly pushed the dissidence of Arius and his followers into prominence, to the point that it soon crowded out all other contentious issues of faith. The ensuing months brought ever increasing polarization of positions, as the opposing camps in the debate took shape.

From his base in Caesarea, Arius traveled extensively throughout Palestine, Syria and the western provinces of Asia, preaching in local churches at the invitation of their priests and bishops. He persuaded several of them to write to others in his support. In an effort to reach out to the masses, he composed a lyrical mixture of poetry and prose in Greek, which he called *The Thalia*, setting out his theology in a form that could be easily memorized, even sung, by common believers who could not read or write and had no use for a copy of the scriptures:

"*God Himself then, in His own nature, is ineffable by all men.*

Equal or like Himself He alone has none, or one in glory.

And Ingenerate we call Him, because of Him who is generate by nature.

We praise Him as without beginning because of Him who has a beginning.

And adore Him as everlasting, because of Him who in time has come to be.

The Unbegun made the Son a beginning of things originated; and advanced Him as a Son to Himself by adoption.

He has nothing proper to God in proper subsistence.

For He is not equal, no, nor one in essence with Him.

Thus there is a Triad, not in equal glories.

Not intermingling with each other are their subsistences.

One more glorious than the other in their glories unto immensity.

Foreign from the Son in essence is the Father, for He is without beginning. Understand that the Monad was; but the Dyad was not, before it was in existence. It follows at once that, though the Son was not, the Father was God.

To speak in brief, God is ineffable to His Son.

For He is to Himself what He is, that is, unspeakable.

So that nothing which is called comprehensible does the Son know to speak about; for it is impossible for Him to investigate the Father, who is by Himself.

For the Son does not know His own essence, For, being Son, He really existed, at the will of the Father.

What argument then allows, that He who is from the Father should know His own parent by comprehension?

For it is plain that for that which hath a beginning to conceive how the Unbegun is, or to grasp the idea, is not possible.

Arius's supporters quickly made sure that *The Thalia* got wide circulation.

In Caesarea, Eusebius Pamphilus, who had long since become convinced that Arius's teachings were both logically coherent and scripturally consistent, was dismayed to see the Arian position mischaracterized by Alexander. Determined to stand with his friend, he penned a response to Alexander defending the Arians:

"Your letters have misrepresented them as though they were saying that since the Son came into being from nothing, he must therefore be just like the rest of creation. But they have brought forth their own document, which they have written for you, in which they explain their faith, confessing it with these very words: 'The God of the Law and of the Prophets and of the New Testament begat an only begotten son before time began, through whom he also made the ages and all things, begetting him not in appearance but in reality, causing him to exist by his own will. He is unchanging and unchangeable, God's perfect creation, but not a creation in the same way like one of God's other creations.'

"And so surely indeed their writings speak the truth, since these opinions are certainly held by you also when they confess that the son of God existed *before time began, that God also made the ages through him, that he is unchanging, God's perfect creation, but not like God's other creations. But your letter surely misrepresents them as saying that the son is the same as the other created things. They are not saying this! But they clearly draw a distinction, saying that he is, 'not like one of the created things.'*

"*Take care, then, lest immediately again a pretext be found for arresting them and keeping them from moving about as much as they wish. Again, you accuse them of saying, 'He-who-was begat he-who-was-not'? I would be astonished if someone were able to speak differently. For if there is only one who exists, it is clear that everything which exists has come into being from him, whatever indeed exists after him. If it were not he alone who exists eternally, but the son also exists eternally, how indeed could one who exists beget another who already exists? It would have to follow that there would actually be two who exist eternally.*"

In Nicomedia, the other Eusebius convened a number of local Arian supporters in an effort to urge Alexander to receive Arius back and restore him to communion. He also continued to write to colleagues throughout the Mediterranean world in defense of the Arian doctrine. Those who sided with him were enlisted for their further aid; those who refused, he chastised; and those who hesitated to take a stand, he chided into action. Prelates in Palestine and Syria he left to Eusebius of Caesarea to recruit, unless the latter asked for his help. Such was the case with Paulinus, the influential Bishop of Tyre, to whom he sent this letter:

"*To my lord Paulinus, Eusebius sends greeting in the Lord.*

"*The zeal of my lord Eusebius in the cause of the truth, and likewise your silence concerning it, have not failed to reach our ears. Accordingly, if, on the one hand, we rejoiced on account of the zeal of my lord Eusebius; on the other we are grieved at you, because even the silence of such a man appears like a defeat of our cause. Hence, as it behooves not a wise man to be of a different opinion from others, and to be silent concerning the truth, stir up, I exhort you, within yourself the spirit of wisdom to write, and at length begin what may be profitable to yourself and to others, specially if you consent to write in accordance with Scripture, and tread in the tracks of its words and will.*

"*We have never heard that there are two unbegotten beings, nor that one has been divided into two, nor have we learned or believed that it has ever undergone any change of a corporeal nature; but we affirm that the unbegotten is one and one also that which exists in truth by Him, yet was not made out of His substance, and does not at all participate in the nature or substance of the unbegotten, entirely distinct in nature and in power, and made after perfect likeness both of character and power to the maker. We believe that the mode of His beginning not only cannot be expressed by words but even in thought, and is incomprehensible not only to man, but also to all beings superior to man. These opinions we advance not as having derived them from our own imagination, but as having deduced them from Scripture, whence we learn that the Son was created, established, and begotten in the same substance and in the same immutable and inexpressible nature as the Maker; and so the Lord says, 'God created me in the beginning of His way; I was set up from everlasting; before the hills was I brought forth.'*

"*If He had been from Him or of Him, as a portion of Him, or by an emanation of His substance, it could not be said that He was created or established; and of this you, my lord, are certainly not ignorant. For that which is of the unbegotten could not be said to have been created or founded, either by Him or by another, since it is unbegotten from the beginning. But if the fact of His being called the begotten gives any ground for the belief that, having come into being of the Father's substance, He also has from the Father likeness of nature, we reply that it is not of Him alone that the Scriptures have spoken as begotten, but that they also thus speak of those who are entirely dissimilar to Him by nature. For of men it is said, 'I have begotten and brought up sons, and they have rebelled against me;' and in another place, 'Thou hast forsaken God who begat thee;' and again it is said, 'Who begat the drops of dew?' This expression does not imply that the dew partakes of the nature of God, but simply that all things were formed according to His will. There is, indeed, nothing which is of His substance, yet everything which exists has been called into being by His will. He is God; and all things were made in His likeness, and in the future likeness of His Word, being created of His free will. All things were made by His means by God. All things are of God.*

"*When you have received my letter, and have revised it according to the knowledge and grace given you by God, I beg you will write as soon as possible to my lord Alexander. I feel confident that if you would write to him, you would succeed in bringing him over to your opinion. Salute all the brethren in the Lord. May you, my lord, be preserved by the grace of God, and be led to pray for us.*"

The plea worked; Paulinus not only wrote to Alexander expressing his agreement with the main points of Arius's doctrine, but along with Eusebius of Caesarea convened a council in Palestine, at which they persuaded a number of local bishops to throw their support behind Arius as well.

Heresy

A further boost to the Arian movement came from a doctrinal treatise authored by the Cappadocian philosopher Asterius, another former student of Lucian, who was popularly known as "the Sophist." Asterius' treatise provided support for the Arian thesis that the Son is himself a creature brought forth by the will rather than the substance of God for the purpose of mediating the rest of creation. It argued that in this respect Father and Son were of one *mind* rather than of one *substance*, and that this was the sense in which John's gospel should be understood when it records Christ as declaring "I and the Father are one." At Eusebius' urging, Asterius traveled extensively through Syria and Asia, publicizing his treatise and speaking to local churches at the invitation of their presbyters and bishops, although he himself was not ordained. Copies in Greek and Syriac were widely distributed throughout the region.

For his part, Alexander became increasingly infuriated by the support Arius was receiving from all quarters. He reacted by stepping up his own pressure on uncommitted prelates throughout the Empire, continuing to write to them, urging rejection of the Arian position. At the same time, he was anxious to secure orthodoxy within his own city and the surrounding regions to prevent further defections to the Arian party. His efforts were only partially successful; in Egypt no less than in Asia and elsewhere, dissension flared, and no central seat of ecclesiastical authority possessed the power to bring the schism under control.

All of these writings back and forth inevitably escalated the controversy to the point where it caught the attention of the one man who was in the best position to resolve it.

Chapter 15

For the better part of a decade, Constantine and Licinius had been feuding over the limits of their respective regimes. Over the years Licinius' increasingly stern treatment of Christians in the East had frittered away whatever initial harmony existed between the two rulers. For Constantine, unifying the empire had become a religious as well as a political mandate, and his pagan brother-in-law stood in the way.

To further his designs on his rival's territory, Constantine stationed the majority of his legions in the Balkans at the eastern edge of his empire, ostensibly to repel the Goths who had recently crossed over the Danube into Roman territory. But that was largely an excuse to mobilize for an attack on the East; the Roman forces were more than twice the number needed to turn back the barbarian invaders. From there it was an easy advance into Thrace—an incursion into Licinius' realm.

In reaction to the threat, Licinius brought a formidable army up to the Thracian city of Adrianople on the banks of the Hebrus River. Constantine promptly countered by advancing his legions and setting up camp on the opposite side of the river. For several days the opposing forces eyed each other across the Hebrus through the thick summer air, each waiting for the other to initiate an attack. Neither army was anxious to risk a river crossing that would expose it to enemy archers, deployed by both sides for several miles along the river.

Finally deciding to take the offensive, Constantine relied on deception to gain his edge. He chose a narrow crossing abutted by a high wooded area where he could hide infantry and cavalry, and then deflected the enemy's attention by amassing ropes and wood further downstream to make it appear as though he intended to build a bridge there. The ruse worked; the bulk of Licinius' archers concentrated on the downstream activity, and Constantine's men managed to pull off a surprise crossing with comparatively little resistance. From there, the rout was on; with a beachhead established, the remainder of Constantine's army quickly crossed at the same point and overwhelmed Licinius' troops before nightfall.

His enemy's forces in hot pursuit, Licinius retreated south to Byzantium with what was left of his army, ferrying most of his troops across the Bosporus to the Asian side but leaving a garrison behind to inhibit Constantine's crossing. He then dispatched his warships down the Sea of Marmara and through the Hellespont, hoping to block Constantine's Aegean navy and thereby forestall both the provisions that Constantine would need for a successful siege of Byzantium and the means for an alternative water crossing by the Roman forces. Neither one of his hopes would be realized. Impeded by a strong south wind, his ships could not make it through the channel in time; the Roman fleet had already arrived in the narrow strait. In the tightly confined naval battle that ensued, Constantine's smaller and more maneuverable ships had the advantage over the unwieldy armada of the East, and destroyed more than a hundred of Licinius' vessels. With the Hellespont now open, convoys could proceed unimpeded to support Constantine's forces.

Having lost control of the sea, Licinius quickly realized that a defense of Byzantium was untenable; Constantine could take the city by siege despite its fortifications, or simply ferry his army across the water and bypass it altogether. Licinius decided to pull all of his troops back and consolidate them at Chalcedon for a final engagement. Constantine's pursuing army crossed into Asia unimpeded, and likewise readied itself for the decisive battle for the eastern provinces.

The opposing legions clashed a few miles to the northeast of Chalcedon, at Chrysopolis, where Constantine launched a single frontal assault under the banner of the Labarum that struck fear into his pagan opponents. The bloody result was a lopsided victory for the invading forces, as thousands of Licinius' soldiers were killed in a single day. The defeated Emperor of the East was obliged to withdraw to Nicomedia with what was left of his routed army, and sue for peace. He dispatched his wife Constantina, half-sister of Constantine, to plead for his life in exchange for surrendering the capital without further resistance. Constantine agreed, sent Licinius quietly into exile, and entered triumphantly into Nicomedia. The civil war

Chapter 15

was finally over. There was one undisputed master of the entire Roman empire—and he was a Christian.

With the military campaign behind him and the empire reunited politically, Constantine was determined to establish a new and lasting *Pax Romana*, and promptly turned his attention to unifying the kingdom in religious matters as well. On taking up temporary residence in the expansive imperial palace while formulating plans for building his new capital at Byzantium, one of his first guests was Eusebius of Nicomedia. The prelate was shown in to the royal chambers by Hosius, Bishop of the Spanish city of Cordova and Constantine's chief religious advisor who accompanied him on all of his military expeditions. When the two bishops entered the throne room, the Emperor extended his hand to Eusebius expecting a kiss of homage, but Eusebius simply bowed respectfully and then stood straight up, his steady gaze directly into the ruler's eyes. Instead of taking offense, Constantine smiled broadly, wagging his forefinger at the visitor with amusement.

"Well, well, bishop! You must be a man of true Christian principles; for I see that they restrain you from displaying fealty to any earthly power—even mine! My predecessor on this throne would doubtless have viewed your actions as treasonable; did you dare to show similar disrespect to him?"

"I intended no insult, Augustus. To the contrary, you are most worthy of respect, as it is clear to all that God's providence is upon you. By his great blessings you have vanquished Licinius, who was no friend to God's holy church. The gospel teaches me no less than to render unto Caesar that which is his. But to God alone must be given the homage due His holy name, for it is solely by His will that all of us, king and commoner alike, live and breathe and have our being—as the Apostle said at the Areopagus."

"You speak the truth, Eusebius. But true it is also that His will is for me alone to live and breathe and have *my* being as His delegated supreme ruler of this earthly world, even as He rules in heaven. God *can* delegate such functions, can He not?"

"Certainly He can, Augustus; He can delegate whatever he wishes to whomever He wishes. Indeed, God has delegated the entire task of creation to His only Son, Jesus Christ. Just as the Apostle wrote to the Corinthians, 'there is one God, the Father, from whom are all things and for whom we exist, and one Lord, Jesus Christ, through whom are all things and through whom we exist.'"

Heresy

"Ah, but tell me, my good bishop; as His delegated ruler here on earth, am I not *also* a son of God, even though vastly inferior to and on an utterly different plane from Christ? For I have lately heard that you likewise profess the doctrine of that rebellious priest, Arius the Libyan, who claims that Christ the Son of God is vastly inferior to and on an utterly different plane from the Father."

Eusebius shot a glance at Hosius, who coyly remained emotionless. So *this* was what his audience with Constantine was about; the Emperor was seeking to bring Arius into line! *You will not find an ally in me, Emperor,* Eusebius thought to himself.

"Arius is hardly a rebel, Augustus—except in the sense of rebelling against unsound doctrine. Is it your wish to discuss the true nature of Christ's relationship to the Father? That may take us some time, although it would be my honor to oblige you."

Constantine's tone suddenly became stern. "You can oblige me by stepping out of the fray, bishop. I have neither the time nor the inclination to indulge such petty philosophical speculations. To me, this unfortunate tumult is all over semantics. My only wish is for unity and peace in the church, yet I see it being divided, at least here in the East, by Arius's and Alexander's theological bickering. The matter has gotten out of hand. Why, even some of my soldiers are professing to follow Arius's views, and there is dissension growing in the ranks! I do not care which side is right, if indeed there *is* a right side. I care more for harmony—as should *all* Christians. Tell me; where is your friend Arius now?"

"He travels extensively. The last letter I received from him was several weeks ago, and if memory serves, I believe he is now heading to Alexandria to visit his old congregation."

"Ah, stepping back into the lion's den, is he? That may be an ill-advised trip, one likely to stir even more controversy. Then again, perhaps having Arius and Alexander in the same place presents an opportunity for mediation. What do you think, Hosius? Shall we urge these two men of God to make their peace?"

"An excellent suggestion, Augusts," Hosius replied with a nod, watching Eusebius intently all the while. Eusebius remained silent. He sensed that the dispute had progressed well beyond the mediation stage, but he could see no point in arguing with the Emperor.

"Let us write to the two of them, then," Constantine said as he rose from his seat, an indication that the audience was over. "Hosius, you will be

Chapter 15

my emissary. Of you, Eusebius, I ask only this: be silent for a time, and hold your tongue and your pen while the mediation effort proceeds. I want no impediments placed in its way."

Chapter 16

The brazen Libyan has returned!

I can scarcely believe it. Alexander stripped him of his parish and made a public show of excommunicating him, yet barely two years later here he is, unrepentant, defiantly strolling through the streets of Baucalis and blithely conversing with the populace as though he were attending a party in his honor! He smiles contentedly as dockworkers greet him warmly and chant verses from his *Thalia* back to him. The Archbishop is incensed, but can do nothing; the civil authorities have no basis to arrest the priest, who commits no crime by his mere presence. If he dares to preach, that could change. But Arius is far too smart for that.

Thus far no reports have come back that he has been replanting his heretical seeds; but of course, what he says in private stays hidden. Still, his very presence is divisive. Every Christian in the city knows he is here, and waits expectantly for the altercation to develop. As do I. It does not happen.

Arius will not venture to show his face at the Catechetical School, but does occasionally visit the library at the Temple of Serapis, where the curator is a friend of mine and apprises me of his comings and goings. I am curious to know whose writings Arius studies while there. The curator tells me "Plotinus," and I scoff loudly, for effect. But I am fascinated, and ask to be shown the specific works. Nearly a century ago Plotinus, like Origen himself, was a pupil of the eclectic theologian Ammonius Saccas here in Alexandria. Plotinus eventually ended up in Rome, where he became the leading philosopher of his day. Because he was a pagan, I have never cared to study his philosophy—until now. The curator obliges me, retrieving the

Chapter 16

scroll and spreading it on the center table in the main hall of the library before returning to his cataloguing duties.

The scroll is a difficult read. Not since pondering the demiurge of Plato's *Timaeus* have I encountered such an esoteric account of the relation between first principles and the intelligible world. Even Plato's work did not rise to this level of detail; Plotinus' teachings are far more refined. Plotinus teaches that ultimate reality consists of a hierarchy of three hypostases: the One (or the Good), which begets the *Nous* (or Divine Mind), from which, in turn, emanates the World-Soul in which all souls and all matter participate and from which they are derived. The One is necessarily simple, necessarily indivisible (if it had parts, they would in turn be fundamental to it and hence the One would not be a *first* principle), and necessarily unknowable (a thing is known by its properties, and the One is devoid of all properties save its own existence). It has no attributes, not even will or intellect, for will implies a duality of willer and things willed, intellect a duality of knower and things known—and the One admits of no duality.

I feel a sudden chill as I begin to realize the significance of what I am reading. The parallels between Plotinus and Arius are unmistakable! Plotinus writes that there can be no participation by the *Nous* in the essence of the One; Arius's *Thalia* suggests that the substances of Father and Son are incapable of being intermingled. Could Plotinus be the source of Arius's denial of consubstantiality between Father and Son?

I read on with a new sense of purpose. Plotinus writes of the One: "*Its definition, in fact, could be only 'the indefinable': what is not a thing is not some definite thing. We are in agony for a true expression; we are talking of the untellable; we name, only to indicate for our own use as best we may.*" This much is not without precedent; Clement of Alexandria expressed a similar notion: "*And if we name it, we do not do so properly, terming it either the One, or the Good, or Mind, or Absolute Being, or Father, or God, or Creator, or Lord. We speak not as supplying His name; but for want, we use good names, in order that the mind may have these as points of support, so as not to err in other respects.*" But what is different in Plotinus is his insistence that no definition can be applied to the One even in theory, not because human limitations prevent us from comprehending it, but because there is nothing—no "thing"—to comprehend. Even the *Nous* does not comprehend it.

Could this be Arius's point at the end of his *Thalia*? That the Son cannot possibly share in the same divine substance as the Father because the Father's substance is unknowable—and if the Son shared it, the Son *would*

Heresy

know it? What insidious blasphemy! It is the very mission of the incarnate Son to reveal the Father, and for that to happen, the Son surely *must* know the Father. Did not Christ himself so declare? Indeed, the Son carries "the exact imprint of God's very being," as the opening verses of the Letter to the Hebrews state. Did not Christ himself assert that whoever has seen the Son has seen the Father?

The sudden insight into Arius' philosophy hits me with the shock of a plunge into a pool of cold water. The analogy is unmistakable; Arius's conception of the Father shares a basic affinity with Plotinus' understanding of the One—wholly differentiated by nature from all creation, having nothing of substance in common with what has been made out of nothing. God is so totally transcendent, so essentially "other" than the created cosmos that no participation in that creation is possible, and the gap can be bridged only by begetting some unique instrument through which creation may be translated. For Plotinus, that unique instrument is *Nous*, and for Arius, it is the Son. To Arius, the Son's relation to the Father is solely as manifestation of the Father's potential creative power, his wisdom, his Logos, and while the Son may be called these things, he is these things not through his own independent subsistence but through the Father's will, created for the purpose of further creation—an intermediary interposed to protect the transcendence of God!

An unfamiliar rage begins to well up inside me as I consider this blasphemous portrayal of a distant and inaccessible God in need of being mediated to creation through a power alien to itself. Arius misunderstands the Son because he misunderstands the Father, whom he dares to cast as impersonal and incapable of any intimate communion with man! He has destroyed the God who made us in his image, who walked in the garden and conversed with Adam! What diabolical heresy! *He must be stopped!*

My pulse races until I am short of breath. I leave the scroll unfurled on the desk and rush out of the library without so much as a word of thanks to the curator. But on reaching the bustling street I freeze, lost for purpose, not knowing which way to turn, bereft of any plan. Trembling and delirious, I squat with my back against the side of the building and then rock forward in sickness, retching violent but empty gulps. Spitting bile and gasping for air, I wipe my mouth and clasp my hands against my head, muttering to myself. Shopkeepers and servants pass by and look at me as though I were possessed, or a madman. And indeed, I *am* mad! I must get my emotions in check if I am to be of service in quelling this insidious plan to undermine

Chapter 16

the Faith. *Calm yourself, Athanasius!* Christ needs level-headed soldiers to do battle with the forces arrayed against his church.

I think of the unshakeable serenity of blessed Anthony, and soon my anger begins to ease. Anger is antithetical to serenity, inimical to that condition of attentiveness that makes prayer possible. And this is unquestionably a time to pray.

I rise, and stagger off to Lake Mareotis.

Chapter 17

At the Archbishop's opulent residence, Hosius was received by Alexander with the respect and honor due not only a fellow bishop, but the Emperor's personal messenger and trusted advisor. The Spaniard likewise bowed graciously before Alexander, and after an exchange of pleasantries in Latin that taxed the limits of Alexander's vocabulary, he announced the purpose of his visit in surprisingly fluent Greek. The letter he delivered, a duplicate of which was soon to be presented to Arius as well, was read by Alexander immediately:

> *Victor Constantinus, Maximus Augustus, to Alexander and Arius:*
> *I call that God to witness, as well I may, who is the helper of my endeavors, and the Preserver of all men, that I had a twofold reason for undertaking that duty which I have now performed.*
> *My design then was, first, to bring the diverse judgments formed by all nations respecting the Deity to a condition, as it were, of settled uniformity; and, secondly, to restore to health the system of the world, then suffering under the malignant power of a grievous distemper. Keeping these objects in view, I sought to accomplish the one by the secret eye of thought, while the other I tried to rectify by the power of military authority. For I was aware that, if I should succeed in establishing, according to my hopes, a common harmony of sentiment among all the servants of God, the general course of affairs would also experience a change correspondent to the pious desires of them all.*
> *Finding, then, that the whole of Africa was pervaded by an intolerable spirit of mad folly, through the influence of those who with heedless frivolity had presumed to rend the religion of the people into diverse sects; I was anxious to check this disorder, and could*

discover no other remedy equal to the occasion, except in sending some of yourselves to aid in restoring mutual harmony among the disputants, after I had removed that common enemy of mankind who had interposed his lawless sentence for the prohibition of your holy synods.

I understand, then, that the origin of the present controversy is this. When you, Alexander, demanded of the presbyters what opinion they severally maintained respecting a certain passage in the Divine law, or rather, I should say, that you asked them something connected with an unprofitable question, then you, Arius, inconsiderately insisted on what ought never to have been conceived at all, or if conceived, should have been buried in profound silence. Hence it was that a dissension arose between you, fellowship was withdrawn, and the holy people, rent into diverse parties, no longer preserved the unity of the one body.

Let therefore both the unguarded question and the inconsiderate answer receive your mutual forgiveness. For the cause of your difference has not been any of the leading doctrines or precepts of the Divine law, nor has any new heresy respecting the worship of God arisen among you. You are in truth of one and the same judgment: you may therefore well join in communion and fellowship. For as long as you continue to contend about these small and very insignificant questions, it is not fitting that so large a portion of God's people should be under the direction of your judgment, since you are thus divided between yourselves. I believe it indeed to be not merely unbecoming, but positively evil, that such should be the case.

For since you have, as I said, but one faith, and one sentiment respecting our religion, and since the Divine commandment in all its parts enjoins on us all the duty of maintaining a spirit of concord, let not the circumstance which has led to a slight difference between you, since it does not affect the validity of the whole, cause any division or schism among you.

As far, then, as regards the Divine Providence, let there be one faith, and one understanding among you, one united judgment in reference to God. But as to your subtle disputations on questions of little or no significance, though you may be unable to harmonize in sentiment, such differences should be consigned to the secret custody of your own minds and thoughts. And now, let the preciousness of common affection, let faith in the truth, let the honor due to God and to the observance of his law continue immovably among you. Resume, then, your mutual feelings of friendship, love, and regard: restore to the people their wonted embracings; and do you yourselves, having purified your souls, as it were, once more acknowledge one

Heresy

> *another. For it often happens that when a reconciliation is effected by the removal of the causes of enmity, friendship becomes even sweeter than it was before.*
>
> *Restore me then my quiet days, and untroubled nights, that the joy of undimmed light, the delight of a tranquil life, may henceforth be my portion. Else must I needs mourn, with constant tears, nor shall I be able to pass the residue of my days in peace.*

When he had finished reading, Alexander was visibly distressed, and realized that he needed to choose his words carefully. He invited his visitor to lunch with him in his garden, and the two men went outdoors to stroll in the midday sun and discuss Constantine's missive as the meal was being prepared. Before Alexander could speak, Hosius came right to the point.

"Let me assure you, Alexander, I am fully in agreement with your theological position on these matters. I have no doubt that Arius is in the wrong here. But the politics of the situation transcend right and wrong theological views on such an arcane subject. Through the grace of God the entire Roman Empire is becoming Christian, and disharmony within the church will inevitably foster disharmony within the empire—a circumstance that cries out for compromise. If Arius agrees, would you be willing to meet with him, under my mediation, and attempt to find some common ground? As you see, that is the Emperor's desire."

"But Constantine does not understand, Hosius. This is not a matter that can be resolved by compromise between Arius and me. It is well beyond that stage now, with many clerics taking his side. Indeed, Arius is now largely a figurehead; the movement he started has a life of its own. More importantly, there is no theological middle ground in this dispute, so any compromise between the two of us would at best take the form of personal silence, just as Constantine's letter urges. But how can men such as you and I remain silent in the face of such heresy? We are bishops, with a sacred calling! As soldiers of Christ we are sworn to defend the faith from corruption."

"No one can ask more of a man than to act as his conscience dictates," Hosius sighed soberly, "nor ask less than that. Yet in this case, the greater good is unity for the sake of spreading the gospel. These Christological debates distract attention from the basic message of salvation that we have in Christ; for who will be attracted to a religion whose adherents fight constantly among themselves even as they proclaim God's peace? *That* should be a matter of conscience as well. Your quarrel is, after all, not over essentials. As John's gospel states, 'For God so loved the world that he gave his only Son, so that everyone who believes in him may not perish but may have eternal life.' *There* is your essential! Nowhere does John suggest that 'everyone who believes in him' must also believe that he is of the same divine substance as the Father. Such a deeper understanding can come later, God willing; but we are in the business of saving souls first and foremost."

"My dear bishop," Alexander replied as they continued to walk side by side, "I am sympathetic to your plea for unity, yet I find that I cannot agree with your proposition. The nature of the Son *is* essential to saving souls. John's gospel opens with a declaration that the *Logos* is God for a reason. Tell me: what is it, precisely, about the *Logos* that we must 'believe in' if we are to attain to eternal life? List for me now, to their irreducible minimum, those propositions that you say it suffices to hold as true for purposes of salvation. Is the divine identity not among them? If it is not—if the Son be not of the same substance as the Father, but a mere creature fashioned out of nothing—we will very quickly be forced to conclude, by a series of ineluctable inferences, that the cross was ineffective to redeem mankind from its sins! And that cannot be allowed. A creature cannot save fellow creatures; only God can. Irenaeus knew this; surely you recall his words: '*He who was the Son of God became the Son of man, that man, having been taken into the Word, and receiving the adoption, might become the son of God. For by no other means could we have attained to incorruptibility and immortality, unless we had been united to incorruptibility and immortality. But how could we be joined to incorruptibility and immortality, unless, first, incorruptibility and immortality had become that which we also are, so that the corruptible might be swallowed up by incorruptibility, and the mortal by immortality, that we might receive the adoption of sons?*' It must surely be so, Hosius. You see no soteriology in Arius's teachings because you have not wrestled with them as I have. Let me assure you, those teachings are far more insidious than your blessed Emperor imagines."

"The commoner cares nothing for ineluctable inferences and complex machinations of logic, Alexander. Simplicity of message is what we must present. That is how the gospel took root initially, and that is how we must cultivate it now. Complicating the issue will only prevent it from being grasped by the rank and file. We will find no further converts if they must all be philosophers first!"

Alexander stopped and turned toward his guest with a wistful look. "You must realize, of course, that this entire discussion is academic if Arius is unwilling to renounce his theories. He will likewise resist any notion that our dispute is over inessentials, and he *certainly* will not agree to any mediation. Never have I met a more arrogant priest! I am afraid that your mission here will come to naught, Hosius. If there is to be any compromise, however slight, it will have to be negotiated in synod, not mediated in private between two men."

"Well, perhaps that is where this dispute is heading," Hosius conceded as the two men sat down to their lunch. "As it happens, the Emperor is planning to convene a synod this coming spring, in Ancyra, to settle the question of the proper date of Easter, among other divisive issues. If no compromise can be reached between you and Arius, perhaps this issue can be taken up then as well."

When they had finished their meal, Alexander asked his visitor if he had ever been to Alexandria before, and on learning that this was the Spaniard's first time on Egyptian soil, offered to arrange a tour. Hosius declined with genuine regret. "Thank you for the offer and for your hospitality, Alexander, but my time is limited, and I am constrained to complete my mission and speak with Arius as soon as possible. Much as I would love to visit your famous pyramids and other antiquities, I intend to sail tomorrow for Antioch, where a new archbishop is to be chosen in council to replace the departed Philogonius. We cannot allow such an important episcopate to fall into the hands of heretics! And now, Alexander, if you would be good enough to provide me a guide to lead me to Baucalis, I must be off to find Arius. Thank you for your hospitality. Pray that my remaining time in the city may be productive." The two embraced, and Hosius took his leave.

Arius proved to be easy to find; his return to Baucalis was the buzz of street conversation everywhere, and all of his former congregants knew where he was staying. In stark contrast to the lavish surroundings at the bishop's residence, Hosius was received by Arius in an austere and dingy apartment, graciously provided by a friend, which served as the Libyan's temporary quarters while in Alexandria. Astonished though he was to receive a visit from Constantine's own prelate bearing a personal message from the Emperor himself, Arius did his best not to display emotion, which surprised Hosius, as indeed it was intended to do. Remaining composed, Arius bowed respectfully and motioned for his guest to sit across from him at the rickety wooden table in the center of the room and share some wine.

With a minimum of introductory explanation, Hosius presented the Emperor's letter, and carefully watched the gaunt cleric's face for any sign of expression as he read silently. None came. When he had finished

Chapter 17

reading, Arius leaned back in his chair and calmly passed the letter across the table toward Hosius. His response was cordial but firm. "Please thank the Emperor for his concern, and assure him that while I understand and respect his plea for unity, he is mistaken in thinking that Alexander and I are engaged in a mere 'intellectual exercise,' as his letter puts it. Our disagreement is over a matter of crucial importance to the unity of the Faith. It is a disagreement over the unity of God himself, and I would not be true to my God or to myself if I were to keep silent. I will pray, and trust in God's providence, that the Emperor will find it in his pious heart to respect a poor priest's position of conscience."

Hosius was genuinely dumbfounded by Arius's response. "Your Emperor, by God's grace the ruler of the entire civilized world, *personally* asks you to forbear from pressing disharmony within the church you both profess to love, and *that* is your answer? Without so much as a moment's reflection? I assure you, Constantine will not take kindly to being upbraided in such a fashion! You had best rethink your stance here, priest! If I return to Nicomedia with this defiant reply, you are likely to feel the displeasure of the most powerful man on earth!"

"Constantine would have no power if it were not given to him from above," Arius paraphrased. "My first allegiance is to my God—as is his, and yours."

Enraged, the bishop sprang to his feet and began shouting, his voice quivering, the veins in his neck bulging. "You dare to compare Constantine with Pilate? Now your insolence offends *me* as well, priest! Alexander warned me of your arrogance, but I was unprepared for its extent. This is outrageous! You . . . you shall . . . I am finished here; this meeting is ended!" Hosius flung the letter toward Arius and stormed from the room, muttering loudly to himself in Latin as he left.

"The peace of the Lord be also with you," Arius replied serenely without rising from his seat, and closed his eyes to pray.

Chapter 18

Antioch's predominantly Christian population, greater than that of any other metropolis in the East, was in turmoil when Hosius arrived. The death of the city's old and respected Archbishop Philogonius, an ally of Alexander against the Arians, had left a vacuum of authority in the powerful See, one that each coalition was determined to fill with its own candidate. Eustathius, likewise a proponent of Alexander's position, was opposed by Paulinus, the *de facto* interim bishop and the candidate favored by Eusebius Pamphilus and several other Arian sympathizers in Palestine and Syria. It was clear to all that the contest amounted to a referendum on the Arian doctrine. So contentious was the impending election that there had nearly been rioting in the streets. Hosius was amazed to see the controversy stirring such passion among the common folk. Constantine was right, he thought; this ecclesiastical rift *was* a threat to peace. Something had to be done, and quickly.

Portraying himself as the envoy of the Christian Emperor, Hosius easily managed to get himself recognized as the master of ceremonies by the nearly sixty eastern bishops assembled in the ancient Antiochene basilica. At the outset he required each candidate to express and explain his allegiance or opposition to the Arian view. He then invited any bishop present who so desired to express his own opinions on the subject. Many of them did choose to speak, enough so that Hosius could easily gauge that the opponents of Arius were in the clear majority—for only three, Eusebius Pamphilus, Theodotus of Laodicea and Narcissus of Neronias, affirmed their belief that the Son originated from the Father but not out of the Father's essence and thus was not co-eternal and unchangeable as the Father.

Chapter 18

Confident of the result, Hosius then announced that following the balloting a statement of beliefs would be drafted and put to a vote as well. Eustathius was elected in the first round by a wide margin, and was promptly invited to join Hosius in forming a committee to draft the statement and present it to the assembly for ratification the following day.

That evening, while the drafting committee labored late into the night, Eusebius met with his two like-minded bishops to strategize on how they might thwart Hosius' transparent plan to condemn their views. Eusebius pointed out that no notice had been promulgated regarding any business to be taken up by the synod beyond the election of a new bishop. "That is our strongest challenge," he urged. "If we cannot convince the majority of the soundness of our doctrine, we must try to dissuade them from adopting *any* statement, on procedural grounds. We have all been ambushed by this, and that is fundamentally unfair. Who can say whether more bishops would have attended if only they knew this issue would be on the agenda, perhaps even enough to turn the tide against the Alexandrian position?"

"I am not convinced that we lack sufficient support to turn that tide, even among the bishops who *have* come to Antioch," Theodotus countered. "True, most of those who declared today did so against us, but not all spoke; and if we can turn even a few of those who announced that they were in the Alexandrian camp, we may yet win a majority. I have to believe that most of those who were silent will line up with us in the end. You know how well regarded Arius's views are here in Syria."

"You are hoping against hope, Theodotus," replied Narcissus. "Have you not counted how many of those who we felt were with us have already gone the other way? It grieves me to admit this, but I must conclude that many have abandoned their own conscience in order to gain favor with Hosius, no doubt hoping that it will translate into favor with the Emperor. May God forgive them! But we will not be able to turn enough of them around even if Hosius allows extended debate tomorrow—and what are the chances of *that* happening?"

"Narcissus is right," Eusebius concurred. "I suspect that all those who will support a creedal statement contrary to Alexander's position are already here in this room! Bishops will not be easily swayed from the positions they have already announced. But those who know in their hearts that they have been less than honest with themselves, and have bended with the political wind, can still save face by agreeing to oppose any formal statement of faith based on lack of notice. Surely that is our best hope." They all agreed to press that objection.

The next morning Hosius opened the synod by calling on Eustathius to read the draft formulated by the pro-Alexandrian faction. As soon as Eustathius had finished, Eusebius rose and made an impassioned plea against *any* vote on the statement, appealing to the gathering's sense of fairness given that no such agenda item had been included in the notice calling the bishops to council. "This is far too important a matter to rush to a vote, my brothers! We have not had the time for reflection, nor for preparation of arguments, nor for the debate that would have attended a proper notice of the issue to be decided—and any statement we adopt today will surely suffer for it. What need is there to ratify a statement of faith here, now, by a gathering that is hardly ecumenical? Is it not better to wait until more bishops, from other regions as well, properly notified of the subject to be decided, can join with us and discuss these issues freely and dispassionately? Indeed, Arius himself is not even here to present his own views!"

"Arius is not a bishop," Hosius shouted in response, "and he has no proper place at this assembly. Besides, his views are already sufficiently known; you and your cohorts have seen to that! As to your concern for ecumenism, we are not purporting to fashion a creed that will govern absent bishops; what we declare here will have no authority beyond our own episcopates. The day will soon arrive when a broader synod will be assembled, one which can proclaim canons for the entire church; indeed, even as we meet here, plans are being made for just such a council in Ancyra, to resolve the dispute over the proper date of Easter. You are free to raise the issue anew in that assembly, Pamphilus, should you choose to be so bold. But we who are assembled here have a sacred duty to lead our own flocks toward the Light, and nothing should be allowed to delay that mission. God demands it. We demand it of ourselves!"

The rumbling of approval that reverberated through the basilica was less a testament to the Spanish bishop's rhetorical skill than to his behind-the-scenes lobbying, for he had privately approached key bishops to persuade them of Constantine's support for any result that would carry near unanimity, as well as of the harsh consequences of being in the minority. Eusebius knew that he was defeated; the only open question was the margin of defeat.

The margin proved to be as lopsided as Eusebius feared. By midday, after a few minor edits, the following statement was agreed upon and promptly subscribed by fifty-six bishops—all except the three who had spoken out in favor of the Arian position the previous day:

> We believe in one God, the Father, the ruler of all, incomprehensible, immutable and unchanging, the providential overseer and governor of all things, righteous and good, maker of heaven and earth and all that is in them, Lord of the Law and the prophets and the New Covenant; and in one Lord Jesus Christ, the only-begotten Son, begotten not out of non-existence, but out of the Father, not as a thing made but as a begotten being in the strict sense, generated in an unutterable and indescribable fashion, since only the Father who begat and the Son who was begotten know its mode—"No one knows the Father except the Son, or the Son except the Father." He always exists and did not earlier on not exist. For we have learned from the holy scriptures that he is the sole image [of the Father], and is not unbegotten, since it is clear that he is, so to speak, 'from' the Father. The scriptures call him a begotten son, in the strict and proper sense—not just by convention, for it would be irreverent and blasphemous to say this. Just so do we believe that he is immutable and unchanging, not begotten or brought into being by will or [only] conventionally speaking, in such a way that he would seem to be generated out of non-existence, but begotten in the way appropriate for him, not in the likeness or the nature of anything that has come to be through him, or mixed with them at all—which it is not lawful to imagine. Rather do we confess, then, because he transcends all conception or understanding or thought, that he was begotten out of the unbegotten Father, God the Word, the true light, righteousness, Jesus Christ, the Lord and Savior of all. For he is the image not of the will or anything else, but of the actual hypostasis of the Father. This Son, God the Word, having also been born and made flesh out of Mary the Mother of God, and suffered, and died, rose from the dead and, when he had been taken into heaven, took his seat at the right hand of the power of the Most High, and is coming to judge living and dead.
>
> Further, as the holy scriptures teach us to put our faith in our Savior, so to they teach us to put our faith in the one Spirit, the one catholic Church, the resurrection of the dead, and a judgment in which everyone will be repaid for what they have done in the flesh, whether good things or bad.

But the addition that came next, inserted by Hosius at the last moment, was utterly unexpected:

Heresy

> *And we anathematize those who say or think or preach that the Son of God is a creature or something brought into being or made and is not truly a begotten being, or that there was when he was not. For we believe that he was [always] and that he is the true light. We further anathematize those who propose that he is immutable by his own free will, and those who introduce the notion that his generation is out of non-existence and that he is not by nature immutable in the way the Father is. For as our Savior is proclaimed to be the image of the Father in every respect, he is so especially in this particular.*

Rising to speak before his attentive peers, Hosius scowled and pointed a finger right at Eusebius, Theodotus and Narcissus, who were steadfast in their refusal to sign. "And as to these three who oppose the truth, let us resolve to have no communion with them until they repent and acknowledge their error, which they will have opportunity to do soon, in Ancyra. We pray that they will. For God does not change, nor does his Son; but God can change the minds of those who come to him with a genuine spirit of humility."

Hosius' strategy was now clear to Eusebius and his fellow Arians: intimidation by threat of excommunication, rather than logical persuasion, would be his means to influence his fellow bishops at the upcoming summit in Ancyra. Antioch had been nothing more than a solemn farce, a test of that tactic—and it had worked to perfection!

Chapter 19

At the imperial palace in Nicomedia, Constantine briefly scanned over the Antiochene statement of faith that Hosius had translated into Latin for him, and listened with concern as the bishop gave a detailed account of his trip. On hearing his description of the methods used in Antioch to gain consensus for the statement, Constantine looked up from the parchment and scowled. "So then, you parlayed the threat of my displeasure into a coerced agreement; is that it? And this Eusebius Pamphilus who was anathematized, he is the chronicler, the historian, is he not? I know of this man, a devout bishop greatly respected and esteemed—yet you saw fit to make an example of *him*?"

"He has become a source of divisiveness, Augustus, the very thing you rightly abhor in the church."

Constantine was perturbed, and not inclined to hide it. "Your desire for unanimity is commendable, Hosius, but surely this was not the right approach. Making back-room promises and threats to the attendees calls the validity of their pronouncements into question. And I agree with Eusebius' protest that lack of notice regarding the issues to be resolved is an insuperable obstacle to any authoritative vote; bishops elsewhere may refuse to recognize the statement for that reason alone. Besides, there was no debate! How can we be sure that some compromise position would not have resulted if only the opposing views had been fully vetted?"

The Spaniard looked genuinely surprised. "Forgive me, Augustus, but I understood you to desire agreement on these issues, regardless of what was agreed upon."

Heresy

Constantine slammed an open palm down on the arm of his throne and shouted angrily, startling the bishop. "I desired *compromise*! It is always the middle ground that has the best chance of commanding the allegiance of the greatest majority. You had better leave politics to me, and confine yourself to religious issues!"

Duly chastised, Hosius remained silent for a moment before responding in a low voice. "And what if a compromise would be theologically unsound, Augustus?"

"Opinions will differ on that as well," replied the Emperor impatiently. "Your own convictions on what is sound doctrine will be matched by equally strong convictions on the other side; and there will be those who favor a middle position as well. Surely the true nature of the Son of God is a question capable of nuanced answer, and therefore of compromised solution. It is not black or white, to be treated like a question of historical fact. And that is precisely why you must retract the excommunication of the three dissenters. Our goal is to *heal* division in the church, not further divide it. Intolerance of competing views is the wrong message to send to the rest of the bishops, particularly on the eve of inviting them to the first truly ecumenical council we are calling to settle this Easter controversy."

"I beg forgiveness if I acted rashly in this regard, Augustus," Hosius apologized with as much sincerity as he could muster, "but even if word of the dissenters' excommunication has spread, I do not see how it can be retracted without signaling a retreat from the Alexandrian position, and that would run counter to your desire to appear neutral. Besides, a retraction would only serve to bring the excommunications to the attention of those unaware of it."

"Both concerns are easily met," Constantine chided. "We will add the Arian controversy to the council's agenda, and our invitations will tacitly retract the excommunications by announcing that Eusebius Pamphilus will be presiding over the Arian faction."

As distasteful as the thought of redeeming Eusebius from his discredited position was, Hosius could not help acknowledging the monarch's political astuteness, even if it was mirrored by his theological naiveté. "An inspired solution, Augustus! Shall we send word to Eusebius that he will be expected to assume a leadership role at Ancyra?"

"Not Ancyra. I have decided that Nicaea will be a more appropriate venue. The temperature is less oppressive, it is easily approachable by land or sea, closer than Ancyra for attendees from the West, and with a proper palace hall for the assembly. Moreover, it is less than two hours' ride from Nicomedia, which leaves me the option to attend as many sessions as my duties here allow. And yes, I want Eusebius informed of my desire that he spearhead the Arian position. That message can be delivered to him with his invitation, which you should prepare at once. I want the council convened this spring. And Hosius," the Emperor added sternly, "make sure the invitations are scrupulously neutral in their description of the issues to be considered. Lay them out, but take care to imply no favor for either side."

Returning his attention to the document, Constantine was puzzled by the closing declaration of Christ's immutability, and questioned Hosius on its meaning. "Where do we find the proclamation of his immutability in the Scriptures?"

"The thirteenth chapter of the Letter to the Hebrews declares *'Jesus Christ is the same yesterday and today and forever.'* As the image of the Father, he necessarily partakes of the same unchanging nature as the Father possesses; for what is begotten of immutability possesses it in equal measure."

"Yet Christ is the very author of change, for he is the agent of creation—as in the passage from Colossians, *'for in him all things in heaven and on earth were created, things visible and invisible.'* How is it, then, that the mutable can be spawned by the immutable? Indeed, it seems to me that Christ's very immutability would preclude his having any role in creation; for no activity at all can be ascribed to that which is immutable. Is it not more logical to grant that the author of change is himself changeable?"

"That is not our faith, Augustus. Christ would not be truly God if he lacked the immutability of the Father. The activity of creation does not gainsay his unchanging nature, for creativity is inexorably within that nature. He is creative yesterday and today and forever."

"Inexorably within his nature, you say. Tell me then, Hosius: has the cosmos existed eternally?"

"No."

"Then what of *before* 'yesterday,' *before* the creation of the cosmos? Surely Christ was *not* creative then—else creation would have always existed just as he did—and so he must have changed at least once during his eternal existence: at the point of his first creative act. Doesn't this weaken your hypothesis of Christ's immutability?"

"I don't think so, Augustus. Christ *was* creative prior to creation; he eternally willed that it would occur at a particular point in time, so it is

83

still proper to think of him as unchanging creator even while creation was still potential rather than actual. That eternal willing process negates any implication of change in the one who wills. As potentiality becomes actuality, there is no contradiction, no change of the creator's immutable nature."

Constantine was dubious. "Potentiality becoming actuality, yet implying no change; is *that* your explanation?"

"It is at least one possible explanation."

"Then why can't we employ the same thesis to the begetting of the Son by the Father? Why not hypothesize that the ingenerate, immutable Father eternally had the potential to beget the Son, but that such potentiality became actuality at some point in time, resulting in the generation of the Son?"

"I think, Augustus, I can give no better answer than that supplied by Origen, in his Commentary on Genesis: '*For God did not begin to be a Father, having been hindered from being so for a time, like human fathers, who must wait to be fathers; for if God was always perfect, and his power of being a Father was always present with him, and if it was good for him to be the Father of such a Son, why should he defer it, and deprive himself of the good from time to time, so to speak, when he might have been the Father of a Son, and was not?*'"

"That is a ridiculous argument, Hosius! If it had any validity, it would apply as well to *all* of creation, which you have already granted did not always exist. If God was always perfect, and His power of creation was always present with Him, and if it was good for Him to create, why should He defer it and deprive Himself of the good from time to time, so to speak, when He might have been the Creator, and was not?"

Hosius fell sheepishly silent at this analogy, realizing that he had underestimated the Emperor's debating skills. Constantine, for his part, looked thoroughly amused. "My dear bishop," he said with a twinkling of the eye, "I think it is time that you warmed to some *other* possible resolutions of this dilemma—including, perhaps, even one suggested by a certain Libyan priest! I want him invited to the council. The man is simply trying to preserve a pure monotheism, free of the philosophical machinations required to make room in it for the divinity of Christ—and that is not an ignoble goal for any lover of truth, no matter how misguided his path may be. The council will give Arius's views a full and impartial hearing."

Chapter 20

For more than a century, controversy had been raging within the Christian church on the proper date for celebrating Easter. The churches in Asia insisted that the date must coincide with the Jewish Passover on the 14th day of the lunar month of Nisan according to the Hebrew calendar, regardless of the day of the week on which it fell. Because Christ's resurrection had occurred on a Sunday, the Roman and Alexandrian churches observed Easter on the following Sunday (if Nisan 14 was not itself a Sunday), or even several Sundays later, after the first full moon following the vernal equinox (if Nisan 14 happened to fall in winter). Both sides agreed that unity in the observance of Easter was vitally important to the church, but neither would concede to the other.

The invitations to the synod in Nicaea, sent in both Greek and Latin to nearly a thousand bishops throughout the empire, listed resolution of the Paschal issue as the first agenda item—but Alexander barely scanned through this opening section of the letter he had received, perusing it instead for the one item that truly mattered to him. *There* it was! While no hint of condemnation could be detected in the missive's brief description of the Arian challenge to the Son's eternity and his sharing in the Father's essence, Alexander was unable to suppress his glee at the prospect of universal censure of his foe. Without so much as a prayer of thanks, he waved the letter above his head triumphantly as he shouted to his servants to prepare for a trip at once. He intended to be among the first arrivals, Athanasius in tow, to begin lobbying for the trinitarian faction.

Three hundred miles away in Caesarea, Eusebius Pamphilus received his own invitation with similar elation, but for different reasons. Pleased that the description of the controversy to be decided was expressed in balanced terms, he was even more gratified that he himself had been requested to take on a leading role in presenting the Arian side. Here would be a measure of personal vindication after the debacle at Antioch, as well as an opportunity to press for a real theological compromise. Without delay he wrote and dispatched letters to Eusebius of Nicomedia and a number of sympathetic Asian bishops, suggesting an advance meeting in Nicomedia to strategize.

In Nicomedia, the other Eusebius was also eagerly anticipating a council quite different from what had reportedly occurred in Antioch. Here, for the first time, would bishops convene from the four corners of the empire, from Gaul to Persia, from Africa to Sarmatia, and for that reason alone their edicts would carry the authority of collective church pronouncements that could legitimately lay claim to divine guidance. Many in attendance, perhaps even most, will not have staked out a position in advance and, he hoped, would keep an open mind. His own episcopate had the prestige to counteract that of Alexander, and he had already worked out the approach he would take in trying to convince the bishops of the West. Determined to take a leading role in favor of the Arian position, he likewise wrote to a number of neighboring bishops favorable to his thinking and suggested a pre-council meeting in Nicomedia.

None of them knew that Arius himself had been invited. The Emperor's letter, delivered to him in Baucalis, came as a complete surprise; he had heard rumors of the synod, but presumed that only bishops would be in attendance. After his disastrous meeting with Hosius a few months earlier, Arius was naturally skeptical of the motive behind this summons, unsure whether he was being set up. He longed for a genuine opportunity to convince open-minded prelates that the Alexandrian deification of Christ was theologically indefensible; but perhaps that was too much to expect. Would he even be allowed to address the assembly, or was he simply to stand for a public indictment? Would his allies rally to his support, or would he be abandoned? The bare chance of the former was enough for him to risk the latter, even if banishment or imprisonment were to follow. At once Arius made plans to travel to Nicomedia and seek the counsel of his old friend Eusebius.

In Nicaea itself, preparations to host the convention were well underway, supervised by Hosius himself. Once word of the upcoming synod spread through the populace, excitement filled the city's Christian community. In the streets and shops, little else was discussed. Christian and non-Christian merchants alike anticipated a boon to their purses, particularly on the news that Constantine had agreed to pay for the lodging and expenses of the attendees out of the public treasury. The imperial palace could not provide sleeping accommodations for even a fraction of all those expected to attend, and rooming houses and inns eagerly awaited the overflow. Vendors of all sorts made ready to ply their wares to the entourages that were about to descend on the city. As the springtime advanced and the warm days grew longer, there was a spirit of pride and optimism throughout this high-walled metropolis on the eastern shore of Lake Ascanius.

On one of his first preparatory visits, Hosius sought and received an audience with Theognis, bishop of Nicaea, who was known to be an Arian sympathizer. The two men were respectful of each other, and if the Bythinian bishop was initially a bit distrustful of his visitor's motives, Hosius quickly managed to put him at ease. "You see from the invitations we have sent out, Theognis, that the Emperor is neutral in this matter and has not prejudged it in any way. He has an open mind on the issues. Whatever the result reached by the council, he is concerned only that the process be fair, and those who wish to be heard on either side of the issue are not stifled."

"I applaud the Emperor's neutrality," Theognis replied, "but in truth, his 'open mind' should be no mind at all. He is not a bishop, certainly not a theologian, and his meddling opinions would hold no sway with me in any event. No temporal authority should have a voice in ecclesiastical matters, much less presume to impart doctrinal clarity."

Hosius nodded his assent. "I am sure the Emperor would agree that it is for the bishops alone to decide the issues dividing us. Theirs are the open minds that matter, and I have no doubt of their collective ability to reach the right decision as long as competing views are articulated robustly and respectfully. That is the key. Time is short, but there is enough time for each side of this theological debate to meet and pray about its presentations. It will be an aid to the deliberations to have more polished expositions of each position. I trust that as bishop of the host city, you will be meeting here in advance of the council with those of the Arian persuasion to discuss their presentation; will you not?"

"Actually," Theognis responded, "such a meeting is to occur in Nicomedia two weeks from today, as I have recently heard from Eusebius. I am not yet sure exactly who will attend; certainly I will be there. But you should be under no misapprehension, Hosius, that any effort will be made to dilute the truth as we perceive it, or to soften its tenor in order to garner wider acceptance."

"I am under none," Hosius said with a calm smile as he rose to leave. "I am sure you and I will see each other again soon. Peace be with you, brother; I must be on my way." The two clasped hands and parted, Hosius' smile broadening once his back was turned to Theognis. *That was all too easy,* he thought to himself as he left. He had confirmed his suspicion of a pre-council gathering of the Arian faction, and now he knew when and where it would be meeting. He already had in mind the man he would recruit to infiltrate that gathering and secretly report back on the strategy being adopted by the opposition.

Chapter 21

The ambitious young Maris had been bishop of Chalcedon for only a short time. Upon his ascendancy to the episcopate through the patronage of Eusebius of Nicomedia, he maintained close ties with his mentor, but he was anxious to make a name for himself and emerge from the shadow of the esteemed primate. His was the first letter of praise received by Constantine from any bishop after the overthrow of Licinius. He had declared his allegiance with the Arian position, but it was widely assumed that this was largely out of gratitude to Eusebius rather than from some deep seated theological conviction. Hosius was optimistic that Maris could be turned into an unwitting ally, although making the overture would not be without risk.

Interrupted from his afternoon prayers, Maris could not restrain his surprise at Hosius' unannounced arrival, which lent a sense of urgency to the visit. Hosius' serious tone simply confirmed the importance of the message he was delivering. "Blessings to you for receiving me, Maris, and please forgive the lack of notice, but I am due back in Nicomedia tonight to meet with the Emperor. I am here because he needs your help."

Something in his visitor's demeanor did not seem quite credible to Maris, but he was intrigued by the notion that Constantine might be reaching out to him, and fought back his suspicions. "I am listening; what can I do?"

"The synod that will soon take place at Nicaea is, as I am sure you know, of the utmost importance to the Emperor. He is a man of faith, and wishes for nothing more than to unify the church and have its bishops end this unfortunate schism. But he desires the ultimate vote to be as near to unanimous as possible. And for that to happen, there must be compromise on both sides of the issue. A defensible middle ground will need to be staked out, and that is more likely to occur if the arguments to be mustered in support of the Arian side can be considered in advance and melded into a compromise document. In short, we need to know the specifics of the Arian defense before the council convenes in order to begin preparing that document.

"We know that in two weeks there is to be a meeting of Arian supporters in Nicomedia to prepare for the synod, a meeting which I trust you will be attending. If we can learn what approach those preparations yield, what scriptural and philosophical arguments the Arian side will be thrusting to the forefront, perhaps we can integrate advance concessions into the Alexandrian position. This will be possible only if we have someone on the inside who agrees to report to us. I have come here to ask that you consider being that person."

Hosius paused briefly to assess the younger man's reaction before continuing. "The Emperor is one who knows how to return a favor. You observe the extent to which Byzantium is being expanded. Constantine intends to establish his capital here. He sees that unlike Rome, its proximity to the frontiers of the empire along the Danube and the Euphrates makes it an ideally strategic seat of government. Within a few years, the city's expansion will be complete and the Emperor will take up permanent residence here. Byzantium will one day become the greatest city of the Eastern empire. Its episcopal chair will be as eminent and powerful as that of Rome or Alexandria or Antioch, soon replacing Nicomedia in importance in this part of the world. And its prelate will be revered throughout the kingdom, with wealth and honor that few bishops have ever known. With the support of the Emperor, that prelate could be you, Maris."

The young bishop tried to assimilate what he had just heard without displaying the rush of emotions that were overwhelming him. Did he hear correctly? Could this be possible? Or was he simply being played for a fool? He looked keenly at Hosius for any trace of an answer in the latter's eyes, without success. "So, you are telling me you need a spy; is that it?"

"Do not think of it in such terms, Maris. What we need is someone who is dedicated to the quest for unity and harmony, in the service of God and of the Emperor."

Maris was dubious, although he tried not to show it. "Why must this be surreptitious? Why don't you simply meet with Eusebius and his

Chapter 21

colleagues in advance of the council, and offer to work out a compromise position directly?"

"Because Eusebius is not *open* to compromise," the Spaniard curtly replied, trying to hide the irritation he was beginning to feel. "He is headstrong enough to think that the Arian doctrine can still command a majority at the council. But in all candor, that is simply unrealistic. Surely you recognize this, Maris. Why, look at what happened in Antioch! The only open question is whether some measure of the Arian position can be recast into whatever statement of faith is ultimately adopted. And the best opportunity for *that* lies in preparing such a statement in advance, by accommodating what is acceptable in the Arian argument in a measured and deliberative fashion. But this cannot be accomplished through guesswork. We must know what arguments will be advanced in order to accommodate them."

"And if I become your eyes and ears in this endeavor, am I to trust that there will be a reward for my efforts?"

"Rest assured, my brother, the Emperor is trustworthy. The question is, are *you*?"

"Clearly *not*, if I am tasked with deceiving the Arian camp!"

"Deceiving it? My dear bishop, nobody is asking you to betray any confidences—for I am sure that none will be reposed in you by Eusebius' group. Surely no one in that gathering will be sworn to secrecy, or even requested to refrain from sharing their collective thoughts with whom they will. If I am mistaken on this, and you feel obliged to preserve confidentiality, then by all means do so. But if you are not adjured to silence, I hope you will do for the Arian caucus what it will not do for itself, and help me to craft an intelligent compromise."

Presented in this light, Hosius' request had some appeal to Maris, but he was still uneasy. He had no desire to disappoint the Emperor by rejecting the assignment out of hand, nor was he prepared to accept it without more careful thought. He needed time to sort this through. "I will consider doing as you ask, Hosius. You will have my answer soon."

"Thank you, brother. I am most grateful for your time, and will anxiously await your response," Hosius declared with a slight bow, and took his leave.

Alone again, Maris saw clearly the precarious position he had been placed in. No matter how it was sugar-coated, Hosius' overture was nothing short of an invitation to treachery—yet to decline it might invite imperial retribution. As he evaluated the possibilities, many questions weighed on him. Would there truly be a reward if he accepted? If he declined, would others be approached with the same offer? Would the outcome of the council be affected by advance disclosure of the Arian strategy, and if so, might it actually redound to the benefit of the Arian position? In his heart he knew that Hosius was right about one thing: the chances of garnering anything approaching full acceptance of the Arian doctrine were remote. Perhaps this truly was an opportunity to salvage something from a difficult job of persuasion. And what could be the harm in making the most of a double opportunity?

With the setting sun coloring the western sky in orange and scarlet hues, Maris threw open the shutters and gazed out his window across the bay, toward Byzantium.

Chapter 22

As the virtual breadbasket of the empire, Egypt shipped prodigious quantities of grain from the port of Alexandria on a daily basis, far exceeding the better known trade in cotton, linen, glass and ivory that passed through its harbor en route to the larger commercial centers of the empire. Wheat was shipped everywhere. On any given day, along its extensive network of wharves that jutted into the harbor like the legs of a centipede, would-be passengers could find a cargo ship bound for almost any city throughout the Mediterranean and its connected seas and lakes—even Nicaea.

The land route from Alexandria to Nicaea was more dependable, but with favorable winds a full week or more could be saved by sailing. Alexander and Athanasius, accompanied by several other deacons and a few servants, decided to split their journey between land and sea by sailing north as far as Attalia, the chief port of Pamphylia, and proceeding across Asia from there, thus avoiding the Etasian winds that sweep down over the Aegean from the north in warmer weather. More importantly, they hoped to use their overland journey, which would take them from Perga up to Pisidian Antioch and through Phrygia, to garner the support of several bishops along the way.

Arius, traveling alone, chose to make the journey entirely by land, through what he hoped would be the bastion of his support in Palestine and Syria. He wondered how many bishops would still be at their sees by the time he arrived. As it happened, he found virtually none; Eusebius Pamphilus, himself anxious to get to Nicomedia, had left Caesarea much earlier, and collected other partisan bishops along his route. *If nothing else,*

Heresy

Arius thought to himself as he proceeded northward, *the synod will be well-attended!*

In Nicomedia itself, the other Eusebius awaited his compatriots and planned for his pre-council summit. He knew that bishops sympathetic to Arius's view were a diverse group with allegiances to different elements of his doctrine. Consensus on the main points would need to be reached if they were to have any hope of standing as one in Nicaea. The results of the recent Antiochene synod would undoubtedly be foremost in their minds. Eusebius needed to find a way to galvanize their support without stirring their fears of excommunication as a penalty for dissent. At the same time, watering down the doctrine to make it palatable to the greatest number could rob it of its value. Maintaining that precarious balance would be a challenge. At its most basic level, any dispute over the divinity of Christ appeared to Eusebius to be a clash of absolutes. Arian-leaning bishops would be well served to explore the extent to which this was so before the main council convened in Nicaea, so that they could present a united approach.

Maris and Theognis were the first to arrive in response to Eusebius' invitation, each of them anxious to begin discussions with their host on that very subject. Their approaches to the issue differed; Theognis was solely focused on analyzing Scriptural passages that argued for or against the Son's eternal generation and essential equality with the Father, while Maris wished to discuss the logic or illogic of such concepts as a philosophical matter. Eusebius favored melding the two. "My brothers," he cautioned, "I have wrestled with both approaches to the issue, as you have. I am convinced that logic and Scripture are not at odds. Scriptural passages on the issue are often ambiguous, and thus require inferences to be drawn from the text, but on neither side of the question are those inferences necessary ones. There is room, indeed there is need, for both exegesis and logic in this debate, and we must be prepared to use both."

"I agree," Maris declared, "but let us not forget that God is rational, and so the Law and the Prophets must be rational and the message of the gospels must be rational. Any ambiguity in Scripture should be resolvable by that principle. Harmonizing the revelation of Scripture with the philosophy of the Greeks is what these Alexandrians are all about, and we must be prepared to meet them on their own terms."

"Using reason and logic is all well and good," Theognis replied, "but the majority of bishops care little for philosophy. Their talisman will be Scripture alone. They will subscribe to a proposition about the nature of

Christ only if it finds support in the text. We must harmonize what is suggested by reason and logic with what we find in Scripture. And we can. Look, for example, at the account in Mark's gospel of Christ healing the paralytic. The scribes who saw blasphemy in his forgiveness of the man's sins reasoned that since only God can forgive sins, Christ must be claiming equality with God. Those who point to this passage as a proof that Christ was truly God are agreeing with the scribes—but who is to say that the scribes' conclusion was correct? Who is to say that Christ was not simply announcing *God's* forgiveness? Cannot God employ an agent to forgive sins on His behalf? Surely the account in John's gospel of Christ commissioning the apostles to forgive sins is clear proof that such agency is possible. *That is the type of argument that will catch the bishops' attention!*"

"You are both right, my brothers," Eusebius interjected as he held his hands up. "Let us step back, and try to accommodate both of these approaches. We must in any event wait for the others to arrive before deciding anything here. But first, let me outline for both of you an overture that I have been pondering for some time as a way to deal with the crucial first chapter of John's gospel. I welcome your opinions." And for the remainder of the day, with the two bishops listening intently, Eusebius set forth his thesis on harmonizing John's understanding of the *Logos* with that of Philo.

Later that same evening, at the imperial palace on the far side of the city, Hosius was dining with Marcellus, the hot-tempered Bishop of Ancyra and an anti-Arian stalwart. Marcellus had made something of a name for himself throughout Asia Minor years earlier, as one of a dozen bishops in synod who had produced what came to be known as the Canons of Ancyra, setting out the conditions of leniency toward those who had renounced the faith during the Diocletian persecution. The two bishops discussed Marcellus' theory that the Arian proof texts regarding the Son's subordination to the Father were applicable only to the incarnate *Logos*, not to the pre-existing *Logos*, and thus presented no serious challenge to the orthodox position. "Go through them all, Hosius," the Galatian bishop insisted, "and satisfy yourself that only after he had 'emptied himself' of equality with God, as Paul's letter to the Philippians puts it, is the Son described as in any way subordinate. Why, even the passage in John's gospel where Christ announces that he is 'ascending to my Father and your Father, to my God and your God,' can be explained in this way. So can they all."

"Well, perhaps not all," Hosius cautioned. "I think your theory may have a difficult time accommodating Paul's declaration to the Corinthians

Heresy

that in the end times, the Son himself will also be subject to the Father. But there is no need for us to rush into a strategy here, brother. We must see how the Arian faction presents its argument, and then decide which formulation is the best response. And I think, in fact, we will gain an insight into that tonight." Marcellus' puzzled look brought a slight smile to Hosius' lips.

As if on cue, there was a short knock on the chamber door, and a visitor was announced by the chambermaid. The visitor quietly walked in to the dimly lit room, and Hosius' smile broadened as he made the introduction.

"Marcellus, I believe you already know the Bishop of Chalcedon!"

Chapter 23

At last, after weeks of travel, we have finally reached Nicaea! In front of the lakeside villa surrounded by majestic chestnut and pine trees that will serve as our dwelling during our time here, Alexander leads us in a brief prayer of thanksgiving for our safe journey and asks for God's blessing on our endeavor. Exhausted from the expedition, he is too fatigued to take in the city today, but I am intrigued by the bustle of activity, and ask for leave to explore while the servants attend to our baggage and prepare our quarters for our lengthy stay.

Staff and purse in hand, I quickly make my way down the narrow stony streets leading inevitably to the Agora, the broad plaza in the middle of the city that serves as the center of commercial and social activity, where I hope to hear the discussions among the natives. As I stroll unobtrusively past the busy storefronts and pavilions, the sounds of merchants hawking their wares from open stalls and tables or beneath tents and awnings rise into a cacophony of cries, calls and laughter emanating from every corner. But many are engaged in deeper discourse than the merely mercantile. My ears strain to catch the subjects of their conversations. I am not disappointed. Putting their daily lives of toil aside, Nicaeans are here mingled by the hundreds in sheer fascination and exuberance over the impending synod. Everywhere the talk of the townsfolk is of the council. The city is packed with visitors, and they too fall easily into conversation with the locals, largely in Greek, again with talk of the synod, and particularly of the Arian controversy, dominating the discussions. While I overhear no debate on its merits, the dispute among the leadership of the church is mentioned again and again, always with eager anticipation of the ultimate resolution, whatever that may be. These simple people know instinctively that the issue about to be decided is one of grave importance to their faith, even if they cannot articulate precisely why.

Suddenly, in the midst of the din and commotion, the noises of the marketplace are eerily muted, almost distant. I hear sounds, but they are filtered, dulled as though my ears have been plunged under water, with the thumping of my own heart beat magnified and pounding in my head. At the same time a dazzling white light pervades the square, one so bright that it forces me to squint. I place my hand against my brow to shield my eyes, but the light penetrates even my hand; it has no source or direction, and cannot be blocked. *What is happening to me?* I can scarcely move, overcome by a sensation of floating, as though suspended in space without the pull of gravity. There is no breath entering or leaving my lungs, yet I feel not the slightest need to inhale or exhale. My skin is tingling. And then, abruptly, I am gripped by an unmistakable sense of spiritual presence.

I have felt this before.

Christ is here! Yes, I can *sense* him. Right here, in this crowded place, Christ is manifesting himself to me!

What an incredible sensation! Many times have I sought him out prayerfully in places of solitude or of natural beauty, away from the distractions of mundane urban routines, only to be frustrated in my effort—but here he is, reaching out to me *right here*, in this busy square, unsolicited! Through these strangers in front of me he speaks, using their voices and turning their entreating eyes toward me. It is their faces I see through the light, but it is Christ himself that I hear, calling out to me in a powerful booming voice as though from out of a tunnel of echoes, yet with extraordinary clarity. He calls:

Protect my lambs, Athanasius!

Yes, Lord; what do you wish me to do?

Protect them!

The surreal voice ceases as abruptly as it began, replaced anew by the babble of the crowd. The piercing white light fades to normal. Disoriented for a moment as though awakened from a trance, I look around me, and see that things are as they were before. Except that my heart is still beating out of my chest!

Puzzlement overtakes my thoughts as I ponder this divine call to action. What, exactly, is Christ asking me to do? How am I to protect these innocent people of faith? Surely that task falls to the bishops; what can a

Chapter 23

mere deacon accomplish on his own at the synod? As I turn to leave the marketplace, I am determined to assist the bishops in any way I can, however the opportunity shall arise, but I remain unsure of what that will entail. All I can do now is trust that this encounter will reveal the means for accomplishing its purpose. Christ has reached out to me; I can only trust that he will again when the time is ripe, and show me precisely how I can be of service. I am dizzy with anticipation as I collect myself and make my way back to the villa.

Moments after my return to our quarters, Hosius arrives; he greets Alexander with a warm embrace, asks politely if the accommodations are to our liking, if we are in need of anything. I can hear a trace of excitement in his voice. He is clearly anxious to begin tactical discussions, and invites us to the imperial palace for dinner and strategizing with like-minded bishops who have already arrived in the city. Alexander graciously accepts the invitation, and as soon as Hosius departs we dress for the occasion. Now it is *I* who am excited, energized by the prospect of being in the company of so many bishops convened in the service of the Lord. My heart begins to race faster as we walk the short distance to the palace. Will Christ's intended role for his humble servant be revealed tonight at dinner? I can only hope.

How fascinating to be in the midst of such a gathering of episcopal luminaries! And how fortunate I am to make their acquaintances; for they all know Alexander, whether personally or by reputation, and he graciously introduces me, as colleague rather than apprentice, in his initial greetings. Many of them bear the marks of sufferings they endured in persecutions, whether through tortures, imprisonment or both. Here was the one-eyed Potamon, bishop of Heraclea in Upper Egypt, who had been sent to the mines and suffered mutilation under Maxentius. Here was Paul of Neo-Cæsarea, whose hands had been rendered useless by destruction of the nerves with red-hot irons after incurring the ire of Licinius. Here was Amphion, Bishop of Epiphania in Cilicia, who had been tortured during the reign of Diocletian. Here also were Spyridion, Bishop of Trimythous in Cyprus, and the famed Bishop Nicholas of Myra, both renowned for their miracles. I am humbled in their presence.

Alas, my hope of meeting Sylvester, the esteemed Bishop of Rome whose influence in the West was as great as that of Alexander in the East, went unmet. Too aged and infirm to travel, he has sent two legates in his stead, Victor and Vincentius, who assure the group that they have been

Heresy

delegated full authority to vote on his behalf. Hosius greets them warmly, in Latin; it is clear that they have met before.

When we sit down to our sumptuous meal, I take a seat next to Alexander, two seats away from Hosius. Our host leads us in a brief prayer, followed by an invitation to the bishops to express their views on the doctrine professed by Arius. Many in the group know little of its details, and as the evening progresses some of those details are expounded and criticized. I listen intently to the discussion but keep my tongue, mindful that I am a deacon among bishops and that Alexander is the one they all wish to hear explain our position. When he does so, it is clear that his words carry great weight among those present; they look to him as the natural leader of the opposition to this heresy. He does not express his opinions in quite the same terms that I would have, but I know my place, and do not presume to supplement his explication. Most of the bishops nod in agreement when Alexander castigates Arius as a heretic.

Hosius surprises us by announcing that Arius himself has been invited to address the council, at the express desire of the Emperor. I sense from his tone that he is not happy about it. Whether the bishops will have full and free opportunity to question Arius is still to be decided, but his views will be heard by the assembly from his own mouth. I glance at Alexander, and note the concern on his face. This is not welcome news. We both know only too well what the rest of them do not: the Libyan is a gifted orator and dangerous debater, not to be taken lightly.

Then Hosius announces yet another surprise, claiming to know the arguments that the supporters of Arius will be presenting at the synod, thanks to an informant. I listen intently as he relates what he has been told—that the many scriptural passages portraying Christ as subordinate to the Father's will are to be offered as proof of the Son's inequality with the Father—and I know at once that he has been deceived. The Arian position is far more sophisticated than this; the Spaniard's informant has thrown him off course in a manner that will have him chasing down scriptural references for days! But again, I keep my tongue. We shall see how the debate plays out. We shall all know soon enough.

The dinner finally ends and the bishops depart cordially, each to his own quarters. To my disappointment, no role for me has been discussed. I am tempted to remind Alexander that allowing non-bishops to address such an assembly is not without precedent, that the Antiochene presbyter Malchion had conducted the investigation of Paul of Samosata in Antioch

Chapter 23

more than half a century ago, but I think the better of it. As I walk with Alexander back to our rooms in the cool night air, I consider telling him of my vision earlier in the day; but he is tired, and tells me that he plans to retire forthwith. We bid each other good night, but I am preoccupied by my experience in the Agora and not ready for sleep despite the long day.

Alone in my room, I pray in silence that Christ will once again speak and illuminate his will for me. Silence is what comes back. Whatever is to be revealed will be on *his* timetable, not mine. It is ever thus. One may distrust whether what seemed to be the voice of God really was; but the reality of God's silence in response to entreaty is unmistakable. Uncooperative reality always feels the more real, nagging in its frustration, leaving the mind with no doubt.

Soon the stillness of the night is broken by the slap of approaching leather sandals, and then by a firm knock on my chamber door. I open it to find Alexander standing in the dim candle light, just bright enough to reveal a peculiar, almost rapturous look on his face. It is a look I have not seen before. "Athanasius," he tells me soberly as he places his hand on my shoulder, "the Lord has spoken to me, just now, with undeniable clarity. It is God's will that *you*, not I, shall deliver the opening remarks for our position at the convention!"

Chapter 24

On the gloriously sunny spring day that the Council of Nicaea convened, some three hundred bishops were in attendance, almost all of them from the Eastern empire. Massive though it was, the palace hall could not contain the bishops' entourages of priests, deacons and acolytes, some of whom were obliged to wait in anterooms, straining in vain to overhear the proceedings. While Greek dominated, the din of the assembly was an acoustical mishmash of languages, as Latin, Syriac, Coptic and many other dialects filled the room.

At the far end of the hall, a gilded throne has been prepared for Constantine. Seating in relation to the throne was blatantly political; the rows of benches and chairs that ran the length of the hall had been carefully assigned by Hosius, who reserved those closest to the throne for bishops he deemed worthiest of positions near the Emperor—Alexander first among them, Athanasius at his side. Those known to be adherents to Arius's teachings were seated at the far end of the hall. The lone exception was Eusebius Pamphilus, who occupied the seat immediately to the left of the throne. Hosius retained the opposite seat adjacent to the throne for himself. Despite their proximity, the two bishops barely acknowledged each other, the sting of Antioch still being felt by each of them.

Abruptly the doors at the far end of the hall were thrown open to the blare of a pair of trumpets, hushing the expectant throng. Every man in the room, even those who were aged or infirm and could do so only with great effort, rose to his feet. Most of them had never before laid eyes on the enigmatic Christian Emperor; some, indeed, had accepted the invitation to Nicaea primarily to see him rather than to debate theology. His entrance

Chapter 24

did not disappoint. Attended by two royal guards, the tall and broad-shouldered Constantine strode into the hall in impressive fashion, wearing a purple and gold robe with the now-familiar *Labarum* embroidered on its chest, the imperial crown adorning his head. As he made his way the length of the room to ascend his throne, the expectant bishops and clergy were respectfully silent, intently watching this beguiling Caesar with the flashing dark eyes, the man who had unified the empire and brought Christianity into official respectability. When at last he took his seat and motioned to the gathering to do likewise, the solemnity of the moment was palpable. Eyeing the crowd without expression, Constantine paused until all had settled into silence again, and then spoke from his seat in Latin, a translator rendering his words into Greek:

"It was my highest wish, my friends, that I might be permitted to enjoy your assembly. I must thank God that, in addition to all other blessings, he has shown me this highest one of all: to see you all gathered here in harmony and with one mind. May no malicious enemy rob us of this happiness, and after the tyranny of the enemy of Christ is conquered by the help of the Redeemer, the wicked demon shall not persecute the divine law with new blasphemies. Discord in the church I consider more fearful and painful than any other war. As soon as I by the help of God had overcome my enemies, I believed that nothing more was now necessary than to give thanks to God in common joy with those whom I had liberated. But when I heard of your division, I was convinced that this matter should by no means be neglected, and in the desire to assist by my service, I have summoned you without delay. I shall, however, feel my desire fulfilled only when I see the minds of all united in that peaceful harmony which you, as the anointed of God, must preach to others. Delay not therefore, my friends, delay not, servants of God; put away all causes of strife, and loose all knots of discord by the laws of peace. Thus shall you accomplish the work most pleasing to God, and confer upon me, your fellow servant, an exceeding great joy."

Tumultuous applause for the Emperor broke out in the hall, and lasted until he finally raised his hands to silence the assembly, nodding in appreciation. Hosius then rose to speak in Greek, informing the bishops that while they had a number of issues to discuss—among them the dating of Easter, the appointment of bishops, the jurisdictional reaches of the sees of Alexandria, Antioch, Jerusalem and Rome, and the transfer of clergy from one see to another—the first topic to be taken up would indeed be the Arian controversy. He announced that Eusebius Pamphilus would introduce the

Heresy

Arian position, to be followed by the remarks of Athanasius, deacon of Alexandria, speaking on behalf of Alexander in opposition, and then by open discussion. All who wished to speak would be heard, he assured the group. The bishops pattered in approval as they settled in with keen anticipation.

When Hosius took his seat, Eusebius Pamphilus stood, peered out into the hall at his fellow bishops and took stock of what he was up against. Setting the right tone, he knew, would be crucial; many of those present were aware of his embarrassment in Antioch, some had even witnessed it firsthand, and it was essential that he reestablish credibility immediately. Although he had practiced his opening speech a dozen times, he prayed that his nervousness would not show. Taking a deep breath, he began:

"My brothers, the cause of Christ brings us together here from all corners of the Empire, and I am grateful beyond words, to God and to the Emperor, for this extraordinary opportunity to convene with all of you in furtherance of that cause. If we can reason together in respectful consideration under the guidance of the Holy Spirit, keeping open and attentive minds until the debates are concluded, I have no doubt that we shall resolve any disagreements among us. I am confident that once we fully understand each others' views on all of these issues, free of the misinformation with which they have been overlain by those who oppose them, we will be guided ineluctably to the truth. And that is so in regard to the questions that have recently been presented by the presbyter Arius, whose position has been much maligned and misrepresented by his opponents, but which it is my now privilege to elucidate.

"It is obvious that the full divinity of our Lord Christ is a concept that presents difficulty for many, if only because the limited support it finds in the Scriptures is veiled in analogy and vague references—and these in tension with our strict monotheistic tradition. That Christ was sired in Mary's womb by the Spirit of God rather than by the sperm of man, thus indicating a relation to the Father transcending that of mere mortals whom he likewise instructed to call upon 'Our Father' but who, in truth, may become sons of God only by adoption, is accepted by all of us. That he was the Word of God and the Wisdom of God, pre-existing his human birth as pure spirit, is similarly granted. But the miraculous birth of a pre-existent spiritual being need not imply a divine incarnation; the leap from pre-existence and transcendent sonship to full and equal participation in the substance of the Father remains a matter of inference rather than of explicit declaration in the Scriptures."

Chapter 24

A faint rumble of discord from across the hall caused Eusebius to pause and scan the room for its source, without success. He raised his voice slightly in response. "But this should not surprise us. Even the earthly Christ was loathe to declare his identity explicitly, pointing instead to the evidence and asking others to draw their own conclusions. When John the Baptist sent his disciples to inquire whether he was the Messiah, Christ did not reply with a simple and unequivocal 'Yes;' he admonished them to report what they saw: 'the blind receive their sight, the lame walk, the lepers are cleansed, the deaf hear, the dead are raised.' Much less do the Scriptures yield a simple and unequivocal answer to the question of Christ's nature as it relates to the Father's. We, too, must search for the evidence from which to draw our conclusions about the relation of the Son to the Father. But unlike the encounter with the Baptist's disciples, Christ has afforded us no visible signs. We are left with only a handful of ambiguous writings, and our own God-given intellect. As Paul's letter to the Corinthians puts it, 'For now we see in a mirror, dimly.'

"And what do we see? Paul's mirror analogy is apt; his epistles contain several passages which refer to the pre-incarnate Christ as a reflection of the Father. To the Colossians, Paul presents him as 'the image of the invisible God,' and to the Philippians as 'the form of God.' These passages tell us that God is made known through the Son as through an image, as an expression of the Father. But it is only through this reflective likeness to the Father that the Son may be thought of as God, as an image of God, a living Son who with the greatest possible exactness mirrors the divinity of the Father. Thus does Christ, as the image of the Father, declare that 'whoever has seen me has seen the Father.'

"My brothers, surely we must all concede that this statement is not a declaration of hypostatic sameness as the Sabellians teach, but merely of likeness and reflection. Image implies no identity of substance. And never does Paul declare such identity. To the Corinthians he distinguishes 'one God, the Father, from whom are all things and for whom we exist, and one Lord, Jesus Christ, through whom are all things and through whom we exist.' To Timothy he proclaims 'there is one God; there is also one mediator between God and humankind, Christ Jesus, himself human.' Paul portrays Christ as exalted by God above all others, certainly; but never does he declare Christ, whom he describes to the Colossians as 'the first-born of all creation,' to *be* God. And no conclusive inference that Paul thought of Christ in that way can properly be drawn from his writings. For if Father and Son were of one substance, they would possess no separate minds or wills—and the Son's obedience to the will of the Father, so often referenced by Paul, would become nonsensical.

"My brothers, it is clear that for Paul, no less than in Christ's own teachings, the distinction between Father and Son remains inviolate. There *is* one God, self-existent and unbegotten. God's hypostasis, God's individuality and uniqueness, that which distinguishes God from all else, is His singularity and unity. They are of His very essence. No begotten Son, whether in the flesh or pre-incarnate, can share in it—for to share in it is to destroy its unity and singularity.

"It is likewise of the essence of God that He is unbegotten. But Christ is *not* unbegotten, and thus cannot be God in any proper sense. Resort to the many scriptural references which speak to the subordination of the Son to the Father is therefore unnecessary. It is the nature of the Father, rather than descriptions of the Son who manifests the Father through imagery, which we will show to be the compelling factor in the Arian approach, and which, in the end, compels the conclusion that the Son as well was created by the Father, existing by the Father's will."

At once the hall erupted in grumblings and stomping of feet, as a number of bishops expressed their disapproval. Hosius let the heckling continue for an uncomfortably long time before rising and holding up his hands to ask for restraint. This was not the line of argument he had expected from the Arian camp. His eyes searched the far end of the room for Maris, whose smug smile let the Spaniard know that his duplicity had been returned in kind. Arius's supporters were not going to be put down *that* easily!

Eusebius resumed when the room had quieted. "In sum, my brothers, Scripture assures us that God is One, but this is more than a declaration that there is but one God; it is a declaration that God is indivisible, that Oneness is of His essence. The true heresy lies in rendering God composite by postulating multiple personhood within Him, for to do so negates His singleness. If God's essence is Oneness, yet Father and Son are equally God, there will be no logical way to account for *any* differences between Father and Son, and we will quickly be thrown back upon the modalist heresy of Sabellius!"

This time the rumblings erupted with even more force. Constantine stroked his chin as he observed the divisive tone in the great hall with concern, silently wondering whether a resolution would be reached before summer.

Chapter 24

Eusebius of Nicomedia was equally perturbed, not by the level of dissension but by the watered down summary of the Arian position that he had just heard. Portraying the Son as perfect image of the Father was all well and good; but why had Pamphilus not seen fit to mention that there was a time when the Son did not exist? Why had there been no explicit declaration that the Son was made out of nothing? It seemed to him that the Bishop of Caesarea was either wavering in his convictions, or deliberately pandering to the opposition in the hope of reaching a compromised statement of beliefs. Of the two, he feared the latter more. Theology, he knew, does not lend itself easily to compromise.

Chapter 25

When Athanasius rose to speak, a deacon before several hundred bishops, the tenor of the room was one of confusion if not discomfort. Most of the attendees, who had not yet made up their mind on the issues, silently questioned why they were being addressed by this youth, this vassal of Alexander, rather than by the respected Archbishop himself. Would not an older, more experienced voice, a voice of equal prestige, be better able to counter the summary just delivered by the respected Bishop of Caesarea? Even Hosius was skeptical of the choice, bowing to Alexander's insistence only reluctantly. But his skepticism dissipated rapidly when Athanasius began to address the congregation with a captivating confidence that belied his years and position.

"My esteemed fathers, I thank Bishop Alexander and I praise God for this blessed opportunity to advocate for the traditions of our church. And blessed it is; for the service of Christ and the shepherding of his flock, which has been entrusted into your hands, can receive no greater blessing than the elimination of schisms that divide us and restoration of the unity that marked the church's beginnings. Such a sacred trust demands affirmation of what we know in our hearts to be true, guided by the Spirit from whom true wisdom comes. And so I, a mere deacon, humbly beg you all to listen not only with your ears, but with your hearts.

"I refer to the traditions of our church with all due reverence. Tradition elucidates Scripture, and confirms its proper interpretation. Every fraud, every heretic, every false prophet who adorns himself in sheep's clothing, but inwardly is a ravenous wolf, weaves his fleece out of ambiguous Scripture verses, quoting them to support his assaults against the true doctrine of the church. It is the tradition handed down from the apostles which fortifies us to resist such strained calumnies, and we do well to adhere to the teachings of those who, in succession to the apostles, are the repository of that tradition. The holy bishop Irenaeus of Lyons knew this; in his renowned work *Against Heresies* he notes: 'Paul then, teaching us where one may find such, says, "God has placed in the church, first, apostles; secondly, prophets; thirdly, teachers." Where, therefore, the gifts of the Lord have been placed, there it behooves us to learn the truth, from those who possess that succession of the church which is from the apostles, and among whom exists that which is sound and blameless in conduct, as well as that which is unadulterated and incorrupt in speech.'

"What, then, is the church's tradition concerning the Son of God? From the very first, the apostles and those who received their doctrine directly from them have understood the pre-incarnate Christ to be both the Wisdom of God and the Word of God as portrayed in the Hebrew Scriptures. Their insistence on this fundamental identity was soon recorded, in gospel and in epistle, identifying Christ with these attributes of God. The saints of subsequent generations then preserved this identity, recognizing that as Word and Wisdom of God, Christ himself could thus be none other than true God. The venerable martyr Ignatius of Antioch, in his *Letter to the Ephesians*, writes of Christ as 'God existing in flesh.' Irenaeus of Lyons writes, once more in *Against Heresies*, that 'He indeed who made all things can alone, together with His Word, properly be termed God and Lord.' Hippolytus, in his renowned treatise *Against Noetus*, writes of 'Christ Jesus the Son of God, who, being God, became man.' The learned Clement, of my own city of Alexandria, writes in his *Exhortation to the Heathen* that 'this very Word has now appeared as man, he alone being both, both God and man.' Such has been our heritage, recognizing Christ as truly divine, as truly God.

"For this reason, from the first outpouring of the Holy Spirit at Pentecost to this very day, Christ has been adored and worshipped throughout his church. *That* is our tradition. Yet we know that to worship a creature is idolatry. Is *that* what we are accused of? It seems that we are; for the followers of Arius insist that Christ is a creature! They point to a verse in Paul's letter to the Colossians which refers to Christ as 'the first-born of all creation,' as though it can be read in isolation. But the following verse tells us that 'all things have been created through him,' and it is obvious that he himself therefore is not part of 'all things'—for he did not create himself!—but rather, as the verse continues, 'he himself is before all things,' preceding all that was made. He is therefore *un*made, *un*created. All things made by him were fashioned from things which were not, but he himself was not so fashioned.

"That the Son was begotten of the Father does not gainsay this, but rather confirms it. There was no point in time at which this begetting took place, as though begetting the Son were an action of the Father rather than an aspect of the Father's being. For he always was, eternally and immutably, the Father; and since being Father necessarily implies having a Son, it follows that the Son likewise was always with Him. Never did the Father lack Wisdom. Never was His Word absent from Him. Thus did Theophilus of Antioch write that 'the Wisdom of God which was in him, and his holy Word which was always present with him.' Thus did Irenaeus write, 'For with him were always present the Word and Wisdom, the Son and the Spirit, by whom and in whom, freely and spontaneously, he made all things, to whom also he speaks, saying, "Let us make man after our image and likeness."' Thus did Hippolytus write, 'He, while existing alone, yet existed in plurality. For he was neither without reason, nor wisdom, nor power, nor counsel.'

"Never, then, was there a time when the Son was not; for though the Son was the agent of all creation, it is manifest that the Son participated in the glory of God *before* all creation. John's gospel quotes Christ praying "Father, glorify me in your own presence with the glory that I had in your presence before the world existed." Not only, then, did the Son exist before the world, but he existed in *glory*. And why, if there was yet no creation by which to glorify the Son? What other source of the Son's glory could there have been prior to creation, except the glory that is due to God *as* God?

"Insofar as there was no time when the Son did not exist with the Father, so too do we believe that the eternally begotten Son must of necessity share in the Father's substance—for if the Son was begotten of the Father *before* all creation, then there was no substance *apart from* the Father's substance from which the Son could be begotten. Eusebius insists that the Father's substance must nevertheless differ from the Son's because the Father is unbegotten and the Son is not; but being unbegotten is not a quality of God's essence missing in the Son. It is not a quality of God's essence at all. Eusebius confuses *how* the Father is with *what* the Father is.

"But more than this, we believe the words of Paul to Timothy which you heard Eusebius recite, that 'there is one mediator between God and humankind, Christ Jesus, himself human.' His humanity does not detract from his divinity. Indeed, if his divinity were not full and equal to the Father's, there could be no mediation, no communication of the divine to the human; for how is it possible that we mortals 'may become participants of the divine nature,' as blessed Peter's second letter states, unless the divine first took on our nature? How can heaven and earth be joined, and our redemption be secured, if the divine does not mix with the mortal? The Arians who hold that the Son does not fully share in the Father's nature do not realize that they thereby strip the Son of power to mediate!

"Such are the slanders with which this assembly must contend. The issues are not hard to resolve, however much they may have seemed so on first inspection; for whatever superficial plausibility attends the Arian position is soon stripped away by closer analysis. Yet in the end, analysis does no more than confirm what we already know in our hearts. We need only search our hearts for the answers that the Holy Spirit implants there. If we do so, there can be no doubt that this sacred body will reach the correct conclusions on the issues before it.

"I pray, finally, for unity. I pray that all present, and all those not present, will abide by the majority's decision, whatever that may be, and unify the church once again in the doctrine which has been its tradition all along. The Emperor's call for unity reflects God's own call for unity in His holy church. And that is our tradition as well. Recall the drawing of lots by the eleven faithful apostles to replace Judas. The Book of Acts does not suggest that Matthias was the group's unanimous choice, but neither does it suggest that those who favored his rival then left the fold. For all that appears in the account of his election, everyone united around the newly chosen apostle. Let us take that as our model, and resolve to do likewise. Then shall the resolutions of this council peal like bells from every corner of the Empire, so that all mankind will know, and forever remember, what has been accomplished here in furtherance of the cause of Christ!"

The great hall was quiet as Athanasius concluded and took his seat. The silence was broken only when Constantine turned toward the deacon and nodded his approval, triggering first applause, and then cheers, from many of the bishops. "Well done, my son," Alexander said as he smiled broadly and placed his hand on the deacon's head. "Well done!"

Chapter 26

Arius paced back and forth while he waited impatiently just outside the great hall of the palace, wishing he could hear the goings-on inside. The guard stationed at the door stood expressionless as he watched Arius, awaiting word from inside to escort him in, and wondering what business this old priest had with the council. Could the man in the worn out tunic before him be the infamous heretic himself, the uncompromising instigator responsible for this synod? He dared not ask.

The entire city was still buzzing from reports of yesterday's stirring speech by Athanasius, and Arius realized only too well that the fragile alliance supporting his views was at risk of dissolving. His eloquence today could make or break acceptance of his views. Eusebius of Nicomedia had cautioned him last night that opportunities to give a comprehensive overview of his beliefs would be infrequent if they came at all, and to take advantage of any opening for one that might arise. The procedure agreed upon in regard to Arius was solely for the bishops to pose specific questions to him, and his opponents would surely not ask open ended ones that invited extended responses. Taking the prelate's advice to heart, Arius had practiced concise summaries of his beliefs through the night, sleeping only fitfully as he played out the possible questions and answers over and over in his mind. But now, as he waited through the morning and into the afternoon, restless anticipation of his interrogation was wearing on him, so much so that he began to wonder if, perhaps, the interminable delay was a strategic move by the Alexandrians.

Finally, word came that the council was ready to hear Arius, and he was brought into the great hall, which fell almost silent as he was ushered

Chapter 26

to a solitary chair in the center of the room. Scanning the assembly he recognized a few friendly faces, but most of the bishops eyed him either with suspicion or curiosity. Seated on the throne at the far end of the hall, Constantine was unmistakable; Arius decided not to acknowledge him, taking his seat without even the slightest of bows. He was surprised to see the Emperor flanked by Hosius and Eusebius Pamphilus, hoping that the latter's seating position signaled balance rather than a defection by a trusted supporter. Perhaps the questioning would disclose which.

"Identify yourself for us, please," Hosius demanded.

"My name is Arius, a presbyter of the holy church of God ordained by Achillas, late Archbishop of Alexandria."

Alexander was the first to rise and address the congregation. "My brothers, I have here in my hand a letter written to me by Arius several years ago. And I now call upon him, in front of this sacred assembly, to acknowledge his words which I now read: that God 'begat an Only-begotten Son before eternal times, through whom he has made both the ages and the universe.' Did you write these words, Arius, and do you believe them?"

"I did, and I do."

"And if the Son was begotten before eternal times, before he himself made the ages, then the Son must likewise be timeless, and therefore without beginning, must he not?"

"Existing prior to time as mankind reckons time does not render the Son without a beginning; only begotten outside of time. But prior to his generation, he did not exist."

Alexander opened his eyes wide for effect as he stretched out both arms to the congregation, raising his voice to the point that it reverberated throughout the hall: "Do you see, my brothers? The man is inconsistent and illogical, speaking in riddles, as though there could be a 'prior' point in time when there is no time at all! What further proof do we need of his irrationality?"

"Will you now tear your clothes and play Caiaphas for us so soon, Alexander?" the bishop of Nicomedia shouted angrily in retort from across the hall. "For you have misconstrued Arius's meaning—or rather, twisted it to your own purposes!"

"What spews forth from this priest's blasphemous mouth, Eusebius, is already so twisted as to require straightening; and certainly *you* are not competent to make it straight! But let us hear from Arius himself; let him defend his own contradictions!"

Heresy

Arius remained calm as he responded. "The Archbishop is correct that there is no prior *time* before time itself was created, just as there are no prior *beings* before any being existed. But the absolute existence ascribed to God gives him priority *in being*, independently of time. His precedence is ontological, not merely temporal. Wherefore he who is unbegotten and ingenerate must of necessity precede that which is begotten and generated, a prior being to the one it begets or generates, outside of time."

"You compound the contradiction, Arius," Alexander rejoined. "Your use of temporal terms 'before' and 'prior' in referring to a being that you say existed *outside* of time forces that being back *into* time! Your declaration that the Son was begotten 'before eternal times' is thus inconsistent."

"There is no contradiction. Eternity is an unending continuity of time, past and future, an infinite series of consecutive moments stretching in an unbroken line in both directions. What comes into being at any point in the continuum, even if it then endures forever, has a temporal existence measured by the line snipped off at one end but not at the other. But the line of time itself, the infinite series of moments, is generated from without, not within; it had no beginning at the back end, for by definition there *is* no back end. God is not dimensional; he is absolutely timeless, transcending time, standing outside of the line of time and thus not measured by it. He begot the Son outside of the line of time as well, and so the Son is likewise not measured by it, having created it from without. In that sense the Father and the Son are 'prior' to time, in the ontological rather than temporal sense. But in the same sense, the Father is 'prior' to the Son. Eternally generated, because begotten outside of the continuum of time, the Son may be; but only the unbegotten Father is *inherently* eternal."

Marcellus of Ancyra then posed the natural next question. "Do you not equate being *begotten* with being *created*, then?"

"To the contrary, I readily acknowledge that they are *not* the same. Creation is always an act of will, whereas one thing can be begotten or generated from another either as an emanation or as a consubstantial portion of its generator—in each case *without* an act of will. But such possibilities apply only to physical things; they are not to be ascribed to God, who is neither physical nor divisible, and whose substance can therefore neither be emanated nor imparted to another being. The Son exists, then, by an act of will of the Father—as any created being."

Chapter 26

An outraged Eustathius spoke next. "This is nonsense! Out of *what* could the Son possibly have been created, if not out of the Father's substance? There *was* nothing else!"

Arius knew that his answer would cause a stir, but he could not back down now. "Precisely. And as nothing existed besides the Father, it follows that the Son was created out of nothing."

Dissenting shouts filled the hall, until Eusebius Pamphilus arose and pleaded with the bishops to allow Arius to finish. "My brothers," he urged, "we have agreed to question this man so that we can hear his views. Let them be heard!" He glanced plaintively toward the Emperor, who took the cue and extended his arms, palms downward, making a slight patting motion with his fingers. At once the rumblings abated.

Arius remained composed and continued when the room had quieted. "You reject the creation of the Son out of nothing, Eustathius, because you deem such an origin to entail some lessening of his power or glory. But there is no reason to assume any such diminution; the Father can empower the Son as fully as He chooses. The alternative of creation out of the substance of the Father presents the greater difficulty, for the unique and ingenerate substance of the Father, by its nature, cannot be shared. If it could, the Father would not be One; there would be a duality or plurality of gods, a notion as blasphemous as it is illogical. We are left with no other reasonable conclusion than that the Son was created out of nothing."

"Ah, but that is where you are wrong, Arius," Athanasius interjected loudly, his lip quivering in anger. "A trinity of *persons* sharing in the unique substance of the one God does not imply a plurality of gods. You deny the possibility of any sharing of that unique substance because you misconstrue its nature. It *can* be shared—even, to some degree, with humanity. The Son can mediate it to us, for he is, as Paul wrote to Timothy and as Eusebius himself noted yesterday, the sole mediator between God and man!"

"A mediator must always be distinct from both parties to the mediation; otherwise, the communication is direct and *unmediated*," Arius calmly rejoined. "If Father and Son are both fully God, you commit yourself to the position that God is mediating with Himself, which is illogical."

"The lack of logic is entirely *yours*, Arius, in refusing to acknowledge the sense of 'mediate' that is possible of a Son with a dual nature, divine and human. *There* is the distinction you blindly reject. It is the *incarnate* Son who mediates, not the pre-existing Son. You should read more of Paul and less of Plotinus!"

Heresy

Eusebius of Nicomedia virtually leapt from his seat in protest to Athanasius' comment. "Arius has been brought before us in order to be questioned, not debated! The debate will be conducted after he has been dismissed, at which time your arguments can be presented to the council. Now, deacon, do you have any *questions* of Arius?"

Athanasius was unfazed. "I have two. Arius, if there be not multiple persons in what you grant to be the one God, how do you explain John's declaration that the Word was God? And how do you explain the Genesis passages which refer to God in the plural, as 'Let us make man in our image and likeness,' and 'See, the man has become like one of us, knowing good and evil;' and others like these?"

The Libyan's measured response took the entire assembly by surprise. "The opening of John's gospel affirms two things: that 'the Word was with God, and the Word was God.' Yet, for one thing or being to be 'with' another there must be some distinction between them. 'Word' and 'God' cannot be identical in every respect, as the Monarchians teach, for otherwise there would be no sense in which God can be thought of as being 'with' Himself. In searching for that distinction, you presume that we must grant either that 'the Word' and 'God' comprise two gods, or else that they comprise two 'persons' joined in one God—and since the first option is heresy, the second must be accurate. You exchange heresy for sophistry; you back into your conclusion as a hypothesis adopted solely to avoid a greater error, but you offer no explanation of its meaning or its logic.

"Likewise, the plural references in Genesis prove nothing about the unique substance of God, nor how it might be divided or shared. A reference to Father and Son acting in unison entails nothing about the relation of the two in regard to their substance. The Hebrew grammar at best supports a plurality of beings, not a plurality of persons in a single God—whatever meaning that concept may hold. The existence of multiple persons in a single being would have been as inscrutable to the Israelites that Moses wrote for as it is to us today, so there is no reason to presume that Moses intended such a peculiar and difficult mental construct in lieu of the ordinary and usual meaning of the words he used, particularly where he offers not the slightest indication elsewhere of any such hidden meaning.

"For that reason, it falls to those who posit a plurality of persons in a single God to prove their thesis. The burden of proof must be on those who argue for such an obscure and esoteric distinction, those who claim a rational explanation for an irrational concept."

Chapter 26

The attentive bishops appeared stunned at Arius's challenge. No further questions were asked, and even the subdued murmurings in the hall quickly died down as the assembly awaited some official retort from the Alexandrians. None was voiced. Doubt had swept into the hall and gained a foothold. The tide was turning.

"You are dismissed, Arius," a flustered Hosius finally announced. "We are adjourned for the day."

Chapter 27

At the conclusion of the day's proceedings, Hosius tasked each side of the debate with forming a committee to prepare a proposed creedal statement for the full council's consideration. The pro-Arian drafting committee sitting around the table at Theognis' residence that evening soon found itself deadlocked, as two strong personalities contended for a leadership role. Both contenders were named Eusebius.

Eusebius Pamphilus and Eusebius of Nicomedia remained cordial as their differences began to surface, the latter's approach being the more hawkish. "We have the Alexandrians on the defensive," he insisted. "They cannot find a rational way to explain their theory of multiple personhood in a single supreme being. It has neither Scriptural support nor logic behind it. The majority will not accept it."

Eusebius Pamphilus was less sanguine. "I fear that my brother underestimates the opposition. They have more potent weapons in their arsenal than Scripture and logic. We would do well to press whatever advantage Arius may have given us by pressing toward a compromise creed. If you will permit me to suggest one, in Caesarea we have for many years recited this confession of faith at every baptism:

> 'We believe in one God, the Father Almighty, the Maker of all things visible and invisible. And in one Lord Jesus Christ, the Word of God, God from God, Light from Light, Life from Life, Son Only-begotten, first-born of every creature, before all the ages, begotten from the Father, by whom also all things were made; Who for our salvation was made flesh, and lived among men, and suffered, and rose again the third day, and ascended to the Father, and will come again in

Chapter 27

> *glory to judge the quick and the dead. And we believe also in One Holy Ghost.'*

My brothers, there may be enough in this to satisfy the Alexandrians, particularly as they will view 'God from God' as a concession."

"And that is precisely why we should *not* present it tomorrow," the other Eusebius objected, becoming more agitated. "It is too soon to offer such a concession. We must leave ourselves a fallback position."

"In normal circumstances, Eusebius, I would agree with you; but I fear we may have only one stab at this. Hosius may well cut any negotiations short, and allow no modifications to the competing positions as they are initially presented. He has the Emperor's ear, and he is on a mission to use imperial persuasion to advantage. I know the character of this man; I witnessed it first hand in Antioch, and suffered humiliation because of it. He means to excommunicate all who side with Arius. Make no mistake: we comprise a jury whose members are themselves being tried. Those who vote to acquit Arius will likely find themselves convicted by their own verdicts. Are we prepared to risk that?"

"I am," declared Theonas of Marmarica, who was determined to support his fellow Libyan regardless of the consequences.

"So am I," added Eusebius of Nicomedia. "I am not interested in compromise."

"That is exactly what Hosius said about you when he tried to entice me to disclose our strategy," a startled Maris responded. "I see he was right!"

"But Pamphilus is right as well," Narcissus insisted. "The risk he identifies is real. It is not philosophical debate which will have the greatest appeal to the greatest number of bishops, most of whom are not well-read or scholarly in their approach to these matters. They will quickly pass over such esoteric arguments as have thus far been presented in synod, in favor of consigning the nature of the Son to the same incomprehensibility as the nature of the Father, regardless of whether they deem those natures identical. We must think of their well-being as well. What if bishops who are unsophisticated in such theological niceties vote our way without appreciating the subtleties being debated, only to find themselves anathematized? Is it fair for us to foist an unanticipated risk of excommunication onto them?"

"You give these bishops too little credit, Narcissus," Eusebius of Nicomedia protested. "They are fully capable of making up their own minds once presented with the alternatives, and will do so with their eyes open. If, indeed, no refinements are allowed to the options presented, the council must at least be given the opportunity to choose the full truth! And if refinements *are* to be allowed, at least we will not have given away too much in our opening position."

"I agree," Maris added. "The possibility that no modifications, no negotiations whatsoever will be allowed is quite remote. A negotiated compromise is precisely what the Emperor wants, and that will surely require more debate and discussion in the assembly. I am confident that we will be allowed retreat to a fallback position if we so choose. But I think, as well, that we should hesitate to so choose. We must not waver in our beliefs just to placate the Alexandrians. And the expression 'God from God' in the Caesarean baptismal formula sounds like wavering to me."

Theonas was even more hesitant. "The expression 'God from God' is not one I am ready to subscribe to, Pamphilus. And I am not sure that Arius would. You yourself told the conclave at its opening session that God's essence is indivisible unity, so how can we think of the Son as 'God from God' without assigning to the Son the status of some lesser god here?"

Theodotus sprang to Pamphilus' defense. "But Christ *is* a lesser god—in the sense that he was like the Father in every respect, a perfect image of the Father, yet not ingenerate like the Father. That distinction preserves the Father's singularity and unity, yet does so consistently with calling Christ a god. Let us remember that the word 'god' as a descriptor has always had more than one connotation. Many times do the Scriptures refer to other 'gods,' the eighty-second Psalm being a prime example. Let it be so as to Christ. Origen wrote in his treatise *Against Celsus* that 'Scripture distinguishes between those gods which are such only in name and those which are truly gods.' Let it do so; we do not need to do so as well. We are free to leave the matter ambiguous, if that is what is required in order for the council to achieve a unified resolution."

"Then it will be a fictitious unity," Maris observed in a low voice, nervously fingering the stem of his cup of wine. "We will seem to be united, yet in our hearts we will remain divided. I don't see the benefit in that. Isn't it better to be divided by truth than united by falsehood?"

"Perhaps," conceded Pamphilus. "But sometimes, the appearance of unity is itself a unifying force, and appearing to limit the disagreement may end up being our strongest selling point. We must at least salvage *something* of the truth from this council. Many in attendance will not be persuaded by logical reasoning if, as I have no doubt will happen, Hosius turns the Emperor against us. By and large these bishops are a simple lot; they will look

Chapter 27

no further than John's declaration that 'the Word was God,' and not bother to parse what 'god' might mean in that context. The phrase 'God from God' may satisfy them. And removal of the phrase will surely be used against us by those in the Alexandrian camp familiar with the Caesarean formula. We will appear to be retreating from our own beliefs."

Eusebius of Nicomedia shook his head. "Perhaps *you* may appear to be retreating, Pamphilus; but only if *you* present the creed. I am happy to make the first presentation of the creed, and afterwards you can supplement it as needed. But we need to be consistent with Arius's answers today. He did a masterful job of avoiding the pitfalls in the opening verses of John's gospel, and we should build on the momentum he has afforded us."

"And how do you propose we do that?"

"I have prepared an argument, largely based on the *Logos* writings of Philo of Alexandria, which Maris and Theognis have already heard, and which I believe will convince many that the declaration in John's prologue 'and the Word was God' must not be taken in the sense of identity of being. If the majority accepts the argument, we will have given your 'God from God' formulation the elucidation it requires in order to avoid ambiguity, and can insert it into the creed if challenged. And if the majority remains unconvinced and we must make a retreat, then the phrase's ambiguity stands, and we will be ready with your backup position as needed. But I see no point in ceding ground to these trinitarians before we are forced to do so."

Dejected, the Bishop of Caesarea gave in with a sigh, although knowing full well that any convoluted argument based on the writings of a Jewish philosopher would never gain traction in the assembly. "Very well, then, Eusebius. Let us hear your argument."

When Eusebius had finished outlining his approach, Secundus of Ptolemais rose to speak. "I find this explanation of the affinity between Philo's and John's use of *Logos* far too esoteric, my brothers; it almost casts the Son as a mere creative utterance of the Father rather than a distinct being with his own subsistence. How are we supposed to wrap our minds around this? I am no philosopher, and neither are the bishops in synod. This will all be lost on them. It is lost on *me*. Rather than debate the fourth gospel's meaning, I propose that we attack the validity of its associating Christ with the *Logos* at all."

"Attack its validity? How do you mean?" asked Maris.

Heresy

"You have heard Eusebius out; now hear *me* out. The *Logos* concept has been a mainstay of Greek philosophy for centuries, but nowhere does it appear in any other gospel, nor in any of Paul's epistles. It is unique to the fourth gospel. No church father so much as mentions the *Logos* until Justin Martyr, more than a century after Christ's death—and even he does not quote from John's gospel, nor even refer to it at all. Indeed, the earliest Fathers display no familiarity whatsoever with John's gospel. Even Polycarp, who was reputed to be a disciple of John, quotes extensively from Paul's epistles, but not once from the gospel we now attribute to John. Not *once*! Surely the tradition that the beloved apostle of the Lord authored this gospel cannot be correct. This gospel represents a late departure from earliest Christian thinking when it associates Christ with the *Logos*. Don't you see? Whoever its author was, he was pandering to the Platonists, reinterpreting the gospel story in terms of Greek philosophy and then attaching John's name to it for prestige! Why must we accept an interpretation that is not grounded in the apostolic roots of our faith? We can declare against it."

The others looked at Secundus with incredulity. There was unanimous dissent in the room, Narcissus' being the most vocal. "Are we so desperate, Secundus, as to reject whatever is inconvenient by attacking its apostolic authority as insufficiently attested? Our tradition is far too well established with regard to the fourth gospel even to consider expressing such a thought! Look at how many of the analogies that John used—Word, Light, Life, only-begotten—made their way into the Caesarean formulation that we just heard Eusebius recite. No, Secundus; we will be instantly anathematized if we take the course you suggest!"

As the bishops continued to disagree on the right approach, one thing was becoming painfully obvious: their own lack of consensus would be fatal to any chance of commanding a consensus at the council. Whatever traction Arius had gained for the group was in danger of slipping away if compromise among his adherents remained elusive, thwarting any prospect of compromise at the synod. Eusebius Pamphilus decided that he needed to give in, despite the risks he perceived. "Very well, then. If we remove the phrase 'God from God' in the Caesarean creed initially, and present the rest of it, holding any reference to Philo's *Logos* theology in reserve, will that suffice as an opening position?"

The other bishops in the room all glanced at Eusebius of Nicomedia, prepared to take their cue from him. After a pregnant pause, he nodded his

Chapter 27

approval: "Let it be so. I will present our opening position tomorrow, and then we can all take part in the debate."

If debate there is to be, a worried Pamphilus thought to himself.

Chapter 28

"Negotiate? *Com*promise? Have you all gone insane?"

To a man, the anti-Arian bishops gathered in committee at the palace that evening to draft their own proposed creedal statement were taken aback by Alexander's vehement refusal to consider any settlement overture. It was evident to all that Arius had acquitted himself well; his suggestion that the onus was on them to prove their insistence on multiple personhood in a single and indivisible God had clearly resonated in the great hall. Some even harbored doubts that such a formidable challenge could be adequately met. But their first order of business was agreeing among themselves on the proper approach—and Alexander's steadfast refusal to give the slightest deference to the Arian position was proving to be problematic.

Recalling Alexander's similar firmness when they first met six months earlier in Alexandria, Hosius knew that the Patriarch would never yield to the group's suggestion that some middle ground be explored. Nothing short of crushing the Arian position would ever command his support. Hosius knew as well that the rest of the bishops would be reluctant to take any stand that lacked Alexander's backing. He had determined to cast his lot with the Egyptian before the session started.

"With all humility, brothers, I must entreat all of you to hear me. Alexander is right. We must not fear to embrace the basic notion that Athanasius so eloquently expressed, and that we all know in our hearts to be true: that the Son is of the same substance as the Father, sharing the same essence. That is what we must proclaim as the center point of our creed, combating the impiety that the Son is a created being. Creator is fundamentally different in substance from creature. For whatever substance is not God is a created substance; and whatever substance is not created is God. If the Son is not consubstantial with the Father, one in essence with the Father, then he is a creature as the Arians claim. We cannot tolerate such a result."

The room fell silent, as the bishops remained hesitant to rally around the *homoousios* banner. Alexander's impatience was evident. "What is it about the notion of Father and Son sharing the same substance that troubles you?" he demanded. "This has been accepted doctrine in my own city for over a century. Clement's commentary on the Epistle of John refers to 'the Son of God, who being, by equality of substance, one with the Father, is eternal and uncreated.' How better can we combat Arius's insistence that the Son is *not* eternal and *not* uncreated?"

"I mean no disrespect to the great traditions of your city and its renowned Catechetical School, Alexander," Macarius of Jerusalem responded, "but Clement elsewhere states that 'the Son is, so to speak, an energy of the Father.' I for one cannot embrace any emanation theories. If we quote him at all at the council, will we not have to defend the *entirety* of Clement's writings? That, I cannot do; and I caution all of you against appeal to any of the church fathers whose teachings we cannot accept as a whole. Why open our sources to impeachment?"

Alexander was resolute. "Impeachment, Macarius? The opening chapter of Clement's *Stromata* declares that he is 'preserving the tradition of the blessed doctrine derived directly from the holy apostles, Peter, James, John, and Paul.' Are you prepared to deny it?"

"Come now, Alexander; did any of the apostles ever once describe the Son as consubstantial with the Father? You know that they did not! The Arian objection to this idea will not focus on whether the writings of Clement support it. The word *homoousios* nowhere appears in *Scripture*, which most of the attendees will agree is itself a sufficient basis from which to elucidate our complete faith. *That* is the impeachment we invite if we focus on this explication of the relation between Father and Son."

A troubled Eustathius picked up the criticism. "It is actually worse than that. You are forgetting that more than half a century ago, the word *homoousios* was disapproved by the Council of Antioch when it condemned the heretic Paul of Samosata. There are more than a few bishops here in Nicaea who will recall this."

"Ah, but Paul of Samosata misused the word," Athanasius replied. "He was referring to the Father being the same *person* as the Son, having no separate hypostasis—what one might think of as *monoousios* rather than *homoousios*. That is not the sense in which we propose to use the word today. *Homoousios* is as apt a word as any to describe the nature of the Son, who could hardy reveal the Father if he were of a substance foreign from that of the Father."

"If you concede that the word can carry two different meanings, then you concede that it is ambiguous," Eustathius rejoined. "Does it affirm the Son's equal deity with the Father, or simply the unity of God in which the Son participates undivided? One can construe it either way—and if the latter, it may be viewed as Sabellian in tone if not in meaning."

"And that very ambiguity may be useful when the time comes for the council to vote," Hosius suggested. "Let each bishop read into it what he will. The more we attempt to refine a formulation, the more difficult it will be to command a majority at the council."

"Perhaps," Macarius objected, "but are we intent on agreement for agreement's sake, or do we seek clarity and precision in our creed? You and Constantine may be willing to sacrifice the latter for the former. I am not. I favor precision. It is better for us to use different words and mean the same thing than to use the same word and mean different things. Besides, do we really need to go so far as to declare the Son's absolute consubstantiality with the Father? I am not persuaded by Athanasius' point that if they are not consubstantial, it would be impossible for the Son to reveal authentic knowledge of God; that no mere creature, however exalted in the realm of heaven, can provide such revelation. Isn't such a position tantamount to declaring that even the prophets have not revealed God? And who among us will believe *that*?"

Athanasius remained unflinching. "I am not suggesting that the prophets did not reveal God; but surely they did so only imperfectly, for they did not know Him as Father, in the intimate way revealed by the Son. Indeed, the Hebrew Scriptures never once refer to God as 'Father.' As Matthew's gospel declares, 'no one knows the Son except the Father, and no one knows the Father except the Son and anyone to whom the Son chooses to reveal him.'"

"I think, Athanasius, you would be well advised to be cautious before quoting *that* verse to the council. If no one knows the Son except the Father, then some may say this synod is a colossal waste of our time in trying to elucidate his nature!"

"You forget, Macarius, that the Father has *already* declared the Son. He did so at the Jordan. He did so at the Transfiguration. He did so at the

Chapter 28

resurrection. We *all* know who the Son is now, and it remains only for us to declare him as well."

Hosius brought the group back into focus. "My brothers, *please*! Time grows short, too short to spar amongst ourselves. We have not much time to draft our creed."

"Why don't we just present the confession of faith adopted in Antioch last fall?" offered Eustathius. "It succeeded there overwhelmingly."

"It is rather too long, not sufficiently succinct," Hosius replied. "And it does not meet the challenge that Arius has put forth regarding the identity of substance as between Father and Son. We *must* insist that the Son is of the same substance as the Father. Let me propose as a starting point the declaration of faith found in the Latin writer Tertullian's treatise *Against Praxeas*, which I have translated from Latin into Greek. Let me read it to you." He produced a small scroll from his robes, spread it on the table in front of him, and held a candle above it as his eyes strained to read aloud:

> *'There is one only God, but under the following dispensation, or economy, as it is called, that this one only God has also a Son, His Word, who proceeded from Himself, by whom all things were made, and without whom nothing was made. Him we believe to have been sent by the Father into the Virgin, and to have been born of her—being both Man and God, the Son of Man and the Son of God, and to have been called by the name of Jesus Christ; we believe Him to have suffered, died, and been buried, according to the Scriptures, and, after He had been raised again by the Father and taken back to heaven, to be sitting at the right hand of the Father, and that He will come to judge the quick and the dead.'*

"Brothers, Tertullian's 'both Man and God' description is fully consistent with the basic doctrine that 'there is one only God,' which everyone at the council is sworn to defend. And Tertullian's writing goes on to state:

> *All are of One, by unity (that is) of substance; while the mystery of the dispensation is still guarded, which distributes the Unity into a Trinity, placing in their order the three Persons—the Father, the Son, and the Holy Ghost: three, however, not in condition, but in degree; not in substance, but in form; not in power, but in aspect; yet of one substance, and of one condition, and of one power, inasmuch as He is one God, from whom these degrees and forms and aspects are reckoned, under the name of the Father, and of the Son, and of the Holy Ghost.*

Here is an explicit contradiction of Arius's position as pronounced by the heretic today. I say we make the most of it. Is there anyone present who cannot subscribe to this statement?"

The bishops grew silent again, glancing uneasily at each other around the room, until Macarius expressed their sentiment. "Whether we here can subscribe to it is not the issue, Hosius. After Arius's presentation today, I fear that the majority will not. Tertullian is not well known here in the East, however well respected he may be in the West. Virtually all of the bishops in attendance at the synod are from the East, and for that reason alone I think we would be better served to focus on an Eastern creed."

As both Alexander and Hosius stared fiercely at the hesitant bishop, Athanasius rose to speak, hoping to break the stalemate.

"Before we present any creed tomorrow, let me suggest an alternative. Hosius, you control the order of proceedings. Why not require the Arian sympathizers to present their own proposed creed first, and then subject it to immediate debate? We can then react to it, and fashion our own in response tomorrow, incorporating what is unoffending and adding the consubstantiality formulation wherever it will find the most suitable position. In this way we will appear to the majority to be yielding to the other side on a number of points even though, in fact, the accommodation will be on nonessentials. Then, we can present our modification as the true compromise creed."

Alexander marveled yet again at his young deacon's cleverness. This was the same approach that Athanasius recommended when Arius had first spewed out his heretical beliefs, and the tactic's wisdom had proven itself then. He gave the approach his unqualified support. "An excellent suggestion, Athanasius! Are we agreed, then, my brothers?"

The mood in the room was discernibly improved, as no dissent was heard. "It is settled, then," a satisfied Hosius declared without formally polling the group. "We shall yield the floor to the Arians tomorrow morning, and urge condemnation of any statement that does not proclaim Christ's co-equal divinity and shared essence with the Father. Pray with me now, brothers, that the synod follows us."

After a brief prayer, the tired bishops rose and made their way to the door, bidding each other good night. Alexander motioned to Athanasius to remain where he stood, and then gently grasped the sleeve of Hosius' robe and leaned in close to his ear. "Stay awhile longer, Hosius," he implored in a low voice. "Athanasius and I require your assistance."

Chapter 28

"For what purpose, Alexander?"

The Archbishop's dark eyes narrowed. "To help us write an anathema."

Chapter 29

When she sent for Arius, Constantina took pains to ensure that her royal half-brother would not find out; she made arrangements to smuggle the priest into the imperial palace under cover of darkness. The hidden passageway was no secret to her. After living at the palace for a dozen years as Augusta of the East, she now lived there as a widow, but with the respect and authority befitting the new Emperor's sister and with complete freedom to move about as she pleased, unquestioned. At her pleading, Constantine banished Licinius to Thessalonica rather than execute him, and she had dutifully followed her husband into exile; but Constantine could not abide the persistent rumors that Licinius was planning an insurrection, and soon had him hanged. Constantina grieved for him but little; their loveless marriage had been arranged as a political expediency, and over the years she had endured his many infidelities with bitterness, and finally resignation. She returned to Nicomedia determined to begin a new chapter in her life and to raise their young son to be a better man than his father.

Constantina was also a Christian sympathizer, and counted Eusebius of Nicomedia among her closest advisors. It was Eusebius who had arranged this evening's clandestine meeting, at her request. Although the bishop was occupied with salvaging as much of the Arian position as possible at the council, he made sure that Arius left Nicaea for Nicomedia promptly after his examination was ended.

The Libyan arrived in the capital as the sun was setting, weary from lack of sleep and from his bumpy trip over the hills on horseback as much as from the stress of his interrogation. Constantina's instructions were flawless; Arius easily managed to slip into the rear entrance of the imperial

Chapter 29

stables next to the palace, unnoticed except by the horses who raised their heads and pricked up their ears but did not give him away. The empty corner stable reserved for his mount was strewn with fresh hay, which he brushed aside to uncover the trap door that led to a narrow tunnel below. He climbed down the ladder and made his way up a slippery stone stairway, illuminated by a single wall torch that competed for what little air was present. With the help of the chambermaid stationed at the top to await his arrival and unbolt the door at his prearranged knock, the out-of-breath priest soon found himself in the presence of the former queen.

Constantina was adorned in a long linen tunic inlaid with gold thread, and sporting a white ribbon diadem around her forehead knotted in the back, unmistakably marking her as royalty. "Thank you for coming, Arius," she said in perfect Greek as she rose from her couch and held out her hand in greeting. "I have heard much about you. Please, sit with me; you look tired. Let me offer you some food and drink." She nodded at her chambermaid, who bowed and promptly left the room. "I trust that today's proceedings in Nicaea went well?"

"That is not for me to judge, my lady. I answered the questions put to me as best I was able; it is in God's hands now."

"Is it? I would have thought it is in the hands of the bishops, whom God appears to be giving free reign to decide His fate, whether as unity or Trinity."

Arius was careful not to display any reaction to his hostess's cynicism. "Do you have a preference as to their decision, my lady?"

"I can abide either one. If you ask me, I think this whole notion of Trinity is just thinly veiled polytheism. But, I suppose, the religions of mankind have always been polytheistic, always embracing hierarchies among gods, demigods and subordinate deities of every sort, each fashioned to deify one relation or another between the divine and the human. The Hebrews alone had some success in resisting this propensity, but it seems that the Christians, although flying the same banner of monotheism, embraced the Gentiles so fully that they soon found themselves assimilating Gentile ways of thinking. They may hold to one ultimate sovereign of the universe, but they cannot restrain themselves from positing all manner of angels and archangels to fill the ancient roles of the demigods, nor from raising up saints and martyrs to correspond to the old heroes of mythology. Some even acknowledge the real existence of the heathens' gods, albeit as inferior and often evil entities. It is as though they have taken the First Commandment

Heresy

'You shall have no other gods before me,' and grafted on to it 'but you may have as many as you wish *after* me.' If Christianity is not as polytheistic as the primitive religions, it has rather strong tendencies in that direction. As far as I can tell, the Trinity is the capstone of those tendencies. I do not pretend to understand the nuances of the three-in-One, but only a fool could fail to observe that the portrayal of Christ as God-man is no novel idea; the religion of the ancients is replete with such beings, the offspring of a divine father and human mother. And as I am a child of that religion, it is easy for me to think of the Son in that context. So if the council decides that the Father and Son share full divinity, the concept will be agreeable to me."

Arius forced a weak smile, too weary to argue. "And what if the council's decision should go the other way?"

"Then I will be happy for you, and for Eusebius. I am no theologian, but I see nothing in your views that should give offense to any right-thinking Christian. And in truth, I think they would give none to the Emperor. But he desires harmony, an end to the constant bickering among the clerics; and he is inclined to follow Hosius' lead on the best way to achieve it."

"Perhaps that, too, is in God's hands. Tell me, my lady; how may I be of service?"

"It is I who wish to be of service to *you*, Arius." She inclined her head slightly closer to her guest. "Two nights ago, I stumbled upon a fragment of what appears to be the Letter of John, in Greek, that Constantine had left on his desk atop his personal effects. There were some notes in the margin in Latin that I believe are in Hosius' handwriting. I am quite sure they have some theological significance to the issues being debated at the council. I dared not remove the fragment, but instead had it copied by my chambermaid, notes and all. How is your Latin?" she asked as she handed a small piece of papyrus to Arius.

"Serviceable enough, I think," the presbyter replied as he began to read the document. Constantina studied his face, which was becoming paler by the second. His hands started to tremble, and he fell shorter of breath as the import of what he was reading became clear. "What is it, Arius?" she asked with genuine concern.

The shuddering Libyan looked up with panic in his eyes, pausing a few moments as he tried to summon the words to respond. His voice cracked as he spoke. "Forgive me, my lady, but I must return to Nicaea. Tonight!"

"Don't be foolish! It is as dark as pitch outside, and the way is treacherous even for the most surefooted of horses. You are not a young man, and

Chapter 29

obviously exhausted from the day's events. When was the last time you had something to eat? Traveling tonight is out of the question; you must stay in Nicomedia until daybreak. The morning will come soon enough."

"*Too* soon, I am afraid. The council will be resuming early, and I must speak with Eusebius before it does."

"No, Arius. If his receiving the document quickly is so crucial, perhaps I can dispatch a courier to deliver this copy to Eusebius tonight." As soon as she made the offer, she hoped he would decline it; there were no couriers who could be trusted to keep such a nocturnal mission hidden from the prefect of the Praetorian Guard, and thus from Constantine.

"It is not the document alone, my lady, but what it signifies that he and I must discuss."

"Then that discussion will just have to wait; making the trip tonight is out of the question. This is no easy journey in the dark. You have not the strength."

Arius knew she was right. The instant adrenal rush that reading this papyrus had injected was now fully overcome by his exhaustion and by the aches of his just-completed trip, which were greatly magnified by his age. A return trip tonight would indeed be impossible. He would simply have to arise early and chance an audience with Eusebius alone at a break in the proceedings tomorrow. "Very well, my lady," he conceded with a deep sigh, clutching the document tight to his chest. "Where may I sleep?"

Chapter 30

From his days as a general in the field, Constantine was accustomed to rising with the sun and taking his breakfast early, outdoors whenever weather permitted. He received Hosius in the lush courtyard of the Nicaean palace before his meal was finished, greeting the bishop in Latin. "Come, Hosius, sit and have something to eat. This is a fine day for healing schisms! What progress with the drafting of a creed?"

"Everything is set, Augustus," the Spaniard replied, remaining standing. "We have one at the ready, but have decided to let the Arian faction present first today. Then we will make appropriate modifications to declare the Son consubstantial with the Father—*homoousios*, as the Greeks put it. I trust that such a formulation would not offend you?"

"My Greek is not refined enough to take offense, Hosius! You say the word means 'consubstantial,' and I am in no position to argue the point, although in truth, I understood *ousia* to mean something other than 'substance.' I understood *ousia* to mean 'being,' the participle of the Greek word for 'to be.' I rather understood the Greek word for 'substance' to be *hypostasis*, *hypo* being Greek for 'under,' conjoined to the root word *sta* which is from the Greek word for 'to stand'—thus corresponding exactly to our 'sub-stance.' Is that not correct?"

"It is, my lord."

"Then why do we so often hear the Alexandrian faction speak of the Son as a distinct *hypostasis* from the Father if, as you say, the two share a single generic substance? Aren't they contradicting themselves?"

"In differing contexts, Augustus, each word can carry differing shades of meaning. The word *hypostasis* can also carry a connotation of 'individual

Chapter 30

subsistence' or 'distinct reality' as well as 'substance.' And the word *ousia* can mean 'substance' or 'essence' or 'stuff' or 'being' or an existence that is concrete as opposed to conceptual—and perhaps more meanings than these. In each case much depends on the context."

"And which meaning of which word is best suited to the task at hand?"

"That depends on how one defines the task. Our challenge is to find a formulation that will not only describe the Son's affinity to the Father with tolerable accuracy, but will do so in a way that cannot be co-opted by the Arians and adapted to their own purposes—something they have proven themselves adept at doing. If we are to rid the church of this heresy, we must find a formulation that drives them into the open. What better way than to use the very terminology they find offensive? Arius's *Thalia* proclaims the Father's *ousia* to be foreign from the Son's, so a proclamation of *homoousios* is sure to expose his supporters. No truly Arian bishop will sign on to a creed that declares Father and Son to be *homoousion*."

"I hope you are right. But using a word with several meanings does seem to put your twin goals in tension."

"Admittedly there is some tension between them; but most of the alternative meanings of *ousia* will serve both purposes."

On hearing this, Constantine leaned back in his seat and revealed a knowing smile. "So for those who find in the word a meaning they can live with doctrinally, at least we will have maximized the level of consensus; is that it?"

"If only everyone were thus enlightened, Augustus! Yes, we hope in this way to minimize the number of dissenters in the synod today. Whether the bishops think of *ousia* as generic, shared being or as distinct, individual being will make little difference. In the end, I am confident that the consubstantiality of Father and Son will secure overwhelming support."

"Precisely what I want to happen, however it happens!"

"Then your own support is crucial, Augustus. Your influence on the undecided bishops is greater than you may think. If the *homoousios* declaration is introduced by you, it will have maximum persuasiveness."

"So be it. I will do whatever will promote a consensus. But let me write the word down in Greek, so that I will be sure to get it right." He called for pen and papyrus, tore a small sliver off the roll, and scrawled *homoiousios* on it.

"Augustus, you have misspelled it," Hosius noted politely. "You inserted an extra *iota* in the middle—and greatly changed its meaning."

Heresy

"Ah; my Greek is still a bit rough. How is the meaning altered?"

"You have changed it from 'same substance' to 'like substance.' Even the Arians can subscribe to the latter!"

The Emperor looked up at Hosius with raised eyebrows and a playful grin, twirling the pen between his fingers. "Well, then, perhaps my slip of the pen is felicitous! Why not present a formulation that will result in unanimity?"

"Because, Augustus, it is only the Son's sharing in the exact same substance of the Father that can truly mark him as God; for it is the substance of the eternal and uncreated Father alone which gives the Son the status of an eternal and divine being rather than a created one."

"Ah. The Son can be begotten, but not created; is that it, bishop?"

"Precisely, my lord. In the Greek, the distinction is between *gennetos*, which means 'begotten' or 'generated,' and *genetos*, which signifies 'having come into existence.' The Father alone is unbegotten and ingenerate, but neither the Father nor the Son 'came into existence,' for both are eternal."

Constantine could not resist a slight chuckle. "So, then, a single *nu* makes all the difference, as does a single *iota*? Greek is no language for the careless! Very well; *homoousios* it shall be." Constantine scratched out the offending letter. "There you are, Hosius. Never let it be said that understanding the true nature of Christ makes not one iota of difference! Come, let us be off; the assembly will be gathering soon."

Chapter 31

Once the doors to the great hall were closed and barred behind the last bishop to enter, everyone in the room could feel the thick weight of anticipation in the air. The usual prattling chatter and small talk that always preceded the official opening of a session was muted; like combatants about to do battle, everyone was intent on the task at hand and not much disposed to prattle. All eyes were cast upon Constantine and Hosius, awaiting the signal for the start of the day's proceedings. It was Hosius who rose to speak.

"Brothers, over the past few days you have patiently considered the arguments presented by both sides of the debate concerning the true nature of the Son of God, and I salute you all. Today, together, we will fashion a creed that incorporates our consensus on the issue. I call upon those who support the Arian position to begin by providing a statement of their beliefs for the council's consideration. So much of it as gains the approval of this body, we shall adopt; and whatever is disapproved, we shall modify until the concurrence of a majority is achieved. Let us begin. Who will be the spokesman?"

Eusebius of Nicomedia stood to accept the challenge in front of the hushed crowd, the Caesarean baptismal creed in his hand. His eyes roamed the room, finding few sympathetic looks on the faces of the bishops. He began to read in a firm voice:

"Our faith is this: 'We believe in one God, the Father Almighty, the Maker of all things visible and invisible. And in one Lord Jesus Christ, the Word of God, Light from Light, Life from Life, Son Only-begotten, firstborn of every creature, before all the ages, begotten from the Father, by whom also all things were made; who for our salvation was made flesh, and lived among men, and suffered, and rose again the third day, and ascended to the Father, and will come again in glory to judge the quick and the dead. And we believe also in One Holy Ghost.' Brothers, we maintain that these doctrines are true, avowing unshakeable confidence in them, and we are prepared to defend them against all impieties. We declare them both necessary and sufficient as a creed of God's church."

Hosius waited for Eusebius to sit before rising and addressing the convention. "Brothers, I trust there is no one here who cannot agree with Eusebius' words as they pertain to the Father and to the Holy Ghost. Let us now discuss his treatment of the Son. Perhaps there as well we will be in general agreement with many of the characterizations we have just heard; for at no time have I heard any dissent to the descriptions of the Son as the Word of God, or as Light from Light, or Life from Life, or as the only-begotten Son of the Father. But what of the description 'first-born of every creature?' Who wishes to be heard on this?"

Eusebius bounced back up from his chair, anger in his voice. "How can there be any question here, Hosius? Paul's letter to the Colossians is explicit that Christ was 'the first-born of all creation.' The Book of Proverbs likewise declares that *'the Lord created me at the beginning of His work.'* Surely any statement affirming this cannot be challenged!"

Alexander was like a coiled snake ready to strike, and immediately pounced on the opportunity to attack his opponent. "If the Son is begotten as you concede, Eusebius, then he is not created in the same sense as other creatures, and we would only confuse the faithful by including both references in our creed. The Son was begotten, not made; the two descriptors are inconsistent. Indeed, the phrase 'first-born of every creature' is itself ambiguous; no one who is born is thereby 'created' in any proper sense. We are born or begotten of our parents, but we are created by God."

Eusebius ceded no ground. "If the phrase appears ambiguous to you, Alexander, it is because you fail to see that 'first-born' is used figuratively, and is not meant to signify a physical birth. The operative concept here is 'created,' which is *not* figuratively employed—and perfectly consistent as a description of the Son's origin!"

"It seems we have a disagreement on this point," Hosius observed calmly. "Very well, then; we shall vote on the matter. Who favors replacing the phrase with 'begotten, not made?'"

Chapter 31

In the shouts that filled the hall, the ayes overwhelmed the nays by a shocking margin. It was instantly clear to all that the tenor of the assembly was overwhelmingly in favor of the Alexandrian position. The Arian supporters looked at each other with panic as Hosius announced "It is so decreed," nodding to his scribe who was scribbling furiously.

Eustathius then rose to address the group. "Brothers, while this modification is an improvement, all of us know what Eusebius' statement lacks: a declaration of the full divinity of the Son. He has been disingenuous. I am familiar with the formulation that he read to us, for it is in use in Caesarea and surrounding regions as a baptismal declaration—and in its original formulation it included the phrase 'God from God,' which Eusebius of Nicomedia has conveniently omitted for obvious reasons. I move that the phrase be restored."

Eusebius of Caesarea's face drained of color as he shot a glance at his namesake. The omission was a grave mistake, he thought, a serious loss of credibility from which they would be hard pressed to recover. Matters were quickly going from bad to worse.

"Let us declare, then, my brothers; who is in favor of restoring the phrase?" Hosius inquired with a grin he could not suppress. This time the affirmative voice vote was even more dominant than before, as several of the Arian-leaning bishops, Eusebius Pamphilus included, replaced their earlier nays with silence, if not ayes. The tide had become a cascade. Hosius decided it was time to strike the decisive blow.

"It remains, then, only to describe the Son's relation to the Father so that we can make sense out of what it means for the Son to be 'God from God.' Who wishes to be heard on this?" His eyes darted at Constantine and then instantly looked away at the crowd.

The perceptive Emperor took the cue and rose to speak before any members of the Arian faction could formulate a response. Their surprise at seeing the Emperor on his feet paralyzed them in their seats and brought the entire hall to complete silence. "If I may be so bold as to offer a suggestion to this assembly," he began in Greek, "I think it important for any creed chosen here today to declare this relation 'God from God' boldly. The choice is yours, but it seems to me that you are leaning toward a declaration which makes sense to me as a layman: that the Son is *homoousios* with the Father, not in any corporeal sense, nor as mortal creatures may share in a particular substance, but in every respect truly of the Father who begat him. I put this forward for your consideration, with all respect."

Heresy

After a pregnant pause, Hosius put the question: "Any discussion?"

A stunned Eusebius of Nicomedia could muster neither strength in his legs nor breath in his lungs to rise and speak against Constantine's suggestion. The other supporters of Arius were equally dazed, holding their tongues while one after another of their opponents praised the Emperor's description as inspired. A few of the Arians muttered "It's not Scriptural" among themselves, but none dared to verbalize the objection loud enough for Constantine or Hosius to hear them. Eusebius Pamphilus simply slumped in his seat and stared blankly into space.

It was over. The Alexandrians had won.

The voice affirmation was a formality. As the great hall hummed in excitement, Hosius waited for his scribe to finish writing, and then took the finished product into his hands and addressed the assembly. "Here, then, my brothers, is our proposed creed:

> "We believe in one God Father Almighty Maker of all things seen and unseen:
>
> And in one Lord Jesus Christ, the Son of God, begotten as only-begotten of the Father, that is of the substance (ousia) of the Father, God of God, Light of light, true God of true God, begotten not made, consubstantial with the Father, through whom all things came into existence, both things on heaven and things on earth; who for us men and for our salvation came down and was incarnate and became man, suffered and rose again the third day, ascended into the heavens, is coming to judge the living and the dead. And in the Holy Spirit."

"We will now vote in it."

"Before we do, my brothers" Alexander interjected loudly, "I have an addendum to propose, one which will unify the church against the heresy that we are about to condemn:

> "But those who say 'There was a time when he did not exist,' and 'Before being begotten he did not exist,' and that he came into being from non-existence, or who allege that the Son of God is of another hypostasis or ousia, or is alterable or changeable, these the Catholic and Apostolic Church condemns."

"My brothers, we must have unity within God's holy church. That is why the Emperor has called us here, and I urge you all to accept that calling boldly, by tolerating no heretics in our midst."

Chapter 31

    Shouts of approval again reverberated through the hall. "So be it," Hosius responded, trying not to appear smug as he directed the scribe to add the anathema.

    Utterly dejected, Eusebius Pamphilus fell silent. *Antioch all over again*, he thought to himself. The fear of expulsion from the church was the same powerful motivator it had always been, inducing believers to stifle their own beliefs. He recalled the twelfth chapter of John's gospel describing the same occurrence among Jewish Christians: "*Nevertheless many, even of the authorities, believed in him. But because of the Pharisees they did not confess it, for fear that they would be put out of the synagogue.*" How little had changed in three centuries! His eyes searched out Theodotus and Narcissus across the room. Would they decline to sign on to Hosius' creed once again, and risk excommunication as they had at Antioch? Would *he*? There was little to gain from obstinacy at this point; but how would he explain himself to his diocese back in Caesarea?

    With Alexander's addendum incorporated, the creed was placed on a writing table in the center of the hall, and Hosius invited all assenting bishops to come forward and sign it. Under the watchful eye of Constantine, the procession to the writing table took nearly an hour. In the end only two bishops, Theonas and Secundus, refused to subscribe to it. Eusebius of Nicomedia and Theognis subscribed to all but the anathema. Eusebius Pamphilus subscribed in full.

    And outside the great hall the entire time, a haggard and desperate Arius, the papyrus from Constantina in his hand, continued to argue vehemently with the guard at the door who steadfastly refused to allow him entry.

Chapter 32

With the council disbanded for the day, Eusebius Pamphilus sat alone in his room and reflected on what had happened, particularly on his own subscription to the creed that had just been overwhelmingly adopted. He had signed on to the *homoousios* formulation despite his well known support for Arius, and there could be little doubt that the Alexandrian party would publicize his concurrence throughout the empire and spin the event as a further triumph for orthodoxy. But what troubled him most were the inquiries about his actions that he was sure to face back home. Many in Caesarea knew he had been selected to spearhead the Arian position at the council, and would see his ultimate agreement to the creed as a reversal. Some were bound to question whether he had sold out his true beliefs in order to avoid a repeat of what had occurred at Antioch. He decided to write a letter of explanation to his diocese:

"You have probably had some intimation, beloved, of the transactions of the great council convened at Nicaea, in relation to the faith of the Church, inasmuch as rumor generally outruns true account of that which has really taken place. But lest from such report alone you might form an incorrect estimate of the matter, we have deemed it necessary to submit to you, in the first place, an exposition of the faith proposed by us in written form; and then a second which has been promulgated, consisting of ours with certain additions to its expression. The declaration of faith set forth by us, which when read in the presence of our most pious emperor, seemed to meet with universal approbation, was thus expressed:

"'According as we received from the bishops who preceded us, both in our instruction [in the knowledge of the truth], and when we were baptized; as also we have ourselves learned from the sacred Scriptures: and in accordance with what we have both believed and taught while discharging the duties of presbyter and the episcopal office itself, so now we believe and present to you the distinct avowal of our faith. It is this:

> "'We believe in one God, the Father Almighty, Maker of all things visible and invisible:—and in one Lord, Jesus Christ, the Word of God, God of God, Light of light, Life of life, the only-begotten Son, born before all creation, begotten of God the Father, before all ages, by whom also all things were made; who on account of our salvation became incarnate, and lived among men; and who suffered and rose again on the third day, and ascended to the Father, and shall come again in glory to judge the living and the dead. We believe also in one Holy Spirit. We believe in the existence and subsistence of each of these [persons]: that the Father is truly Father, the Son truly Son, and the Holy Spirit truly Holy Spirit; even as our Lord also, when he sent forth his disciples to preach the Gospel, said, 'Go and teach all nations, baptizing them in the name of the Father, and of the Son, and of the Holy Spirit.' Concerning these doctrines we steadfastly maintain their truth, and avow our full confidence in them; such also have been our sentiments hitherto, and such we shall continue to hold until death and in an unshaken adherence to this faith, we anathematize every impious heresy. In the presence of God Almighty, and of our Lord Jesus Christ we testify, that thus we have believed and thought from our heart and soul, since we have possessed a right estimate of ourselves; and that we now think and speak what is perfectly in accordance with the truth. We are moreover prepared to prove to you by undeniable evidences, and to convince you that in time past we have thus believed, and so preached.'"

"When these articles of faith were proposed, there seemed to be no ground of opposition: nay, our most pious emperor himself was the first to admit that they were perfectly correct, and that he himself had entertained the sentiments contained in them; exhorting all present to give them their assent, and subscribe to these very articles, thus agreeing in a unanimous profession of them, with the insertion, however, of that single word 'homoousios' (consubstantial), an expression which the emperor himself explained, as not indicating corporeal affections or properties; and consequently that the Son did not subsist from the Father either by division or abscission: for said he, a nature which is immaterial and incorporeal cannot possibly be subject to any corporeal affection; hence our conception of such things can only be in divine and mysterious terms. Such was the philosophical view of the subject taken *by our most wise and pious sovereign; and the bishops on account of the word 'homoousios' drew up this formula of faith:*

> "'We believe in one God, the Father Almighty, Maker of all things visible and invisible:—and in one Lord Jesus Christ, the Son of God, the only-begotten of the Father, that is of the substance of the Father; God of God, Light of light, true God of true God; begotten not made, consubstantial with the Father; by whom all things were made both which are in heaven and on earth; who for the sake of us men, and on account of our salvation, descended, became incarnate, was made man, suffered and rose again on the third day; he ascended into the heavens, and will come to judge the living and the dead. [We believe] also in the Holy Spirit. But those who say 'There was a time when he was not,' or 'He did not exist before he was begotten,' or 'He was made of nothing' or assert that 'He is of other substance or essence than the Father,' or that the Son of God is created, or mutable, or susceptible of change, the Catholic and apostolic Church of God anathematizes."

"*Now this declaration of faith being propounded by them, we did not neglect to investigate the distinct sense of the expressions 'of the substance of the Father, and consubstantial with the Father.' Whereupon questions were put forth and answers, and the meaning of these terms was clearly defined; when it was generally admitted that* ousias *(of the essence or substance) simply implied that the Son is of the Father indeed, but does not subsist as a part of the Father. To this interpretation of the sacred doctrine which declares that the Son is of the Father, but is not a part of his substance, it seemed right to us to assent. We ourselves therefore concurred in this exposition; nor do we cavil at the word 'homoousios' having regard to peace, and fearing to lose a right understanding of the matter.*

"*On the same grounds we admitted also the expression 'begotten, not made': 'for made,' said they, 'is a term applicable in common to all the creatures which were made by the Son, to whom the Son has no resemblance. Consequently he is no creature like those which were made by him, but is of a substance far excelling any creature; which substance the Divine Oracles teach was begotten of the Father by such a mode of generation as cannot be explained nor even conceived by any creature.' Thus also the declaration that 'the Son is consubstantial with the Father' having been discussed, it was agreed that this must not be understood in a corporeal sense, or in any way analogous to mortal creatures; inasmuch as it is neither by division of substance, nor by abscission nor by any change of the Father's substance and power, since the underived nature of the Father is inconsistent with all these things. That he is consubstantial with the Father then simply implies, that the Son of God has no resemblance to created things, but is in every respect like the Father only who begat him; and that he is of no other substance or essence but of the Father. To which doctrine, explained in this way, it appeared right to assent, especially since we knew that some eminent bishops and learned writers among the ancients have used the term 'homoousios' in their theological discourses concerning the nature of the Father and the Son. Such is what I have to state to you in reference to the articles of faith which have been promulgated; and in which we have all concurred, not without due examination, but according to the senses assigned, which were investigated in the presence of our most highly favored emperor, and for the reasons mentioned approved. We have also considered the anathema pronounced by them after the declaration of faith inoffensive; because it prohibits the use of illegitimate terms, from which almost all the distraction and commotion of the churches have arisen. Accordingly, since no divinely inspired Scripture contains the expressions, 'of things which do not exist,' and 'there was a time when he was not,' and such other phrases as are therein subjoined, it seemed unwarrantable to utter and teach them: and moreover this decision received our sanction the rather from the consideration that we have never heretofore been accustomed to employ these terms.*

"*We deemed it incumbent on us, beloved, to acquaint you with the caution which has characterized both our examination of and concurrence in these things: and that on justifiable grounds we resisted to the last moment the introduction of certain objectionable expressions as long as these were not acceptable; and received them without dispute, when on mature deliberation as we examined the sense of the words, they appeared to agree with what we had originally proposed as a sound confession of faith.*"

When he had finished, Eusebius read through his letter again. Not the most convincing explanation, he thought. It was surely disingenuous of him to defend the condemnation of Arian expressions on grounds that they were not found in Scripture, when the same was true of *homoousios*. But it would have to do. Regardless of spin, no explanation for his actions would be fully convincing. Staking out a middle ground had become a matter of trading on ambiguities. And that middle ground was shrinking.

Chapter 33

With the most contentious issue before the synod resolved, Constantine decided to absent himself for a time and return to the imperial palace in Nicomedia. There was, after all, an empire to be ruled, and he had laid civic duties aside long enough. But he could not dismiss the events of the day from his mind, and after a restless night's sleep he promptly dispatched a rider back to Nicaea to summon Hosius for further discussion.

The bishop arrived in the Emperor's chambers at the noon hour to find Constantine perplexed, a copy of the creed in his hand. Without giving the Spaniard an opportunity even to cross the room and bow in greeting, Constantine accosted him as soon as he came through the door. "Why wasn't Alexander's anathema discussed with me in advance?" he demanded. "That was no trifling matter. I should have been informed."

The Emperor's harsh tone caught Hosius off guard, stopping him in his tracks. "My apologies, Augustus. He approached me with it only the night before. I should have called it to your attention. But I do think it was a necessary element of the creed. A statement of beliefs that merely declares the sense of the synod, with no sanctions imposed for deviations, would have rendered the entire creed little more than an advisory opinion."

"Oh, I agree with you there. But my concern is with the wording. It's ambiguous." He glanced at the document. "The anathema denounces those who say 'that the Son of God was of a different *hypostasis* or *ousia*' than the Father. Again, please forgive my limited Greek, but didn't we discuss the different shades of meaning in those words just yesterday? They are not equivalent terms; you yourself assured me of that. I understood your view, and that of the Alexandrians, to be that the Son shared the same *ousia* of

Chapter 33

the Father, the same divine 'substance,' but did indeed have a separate and unique *hypostasis*, which you cautioned me *not* to construe as 'substance.' How, then, can the council now condemn those who say that the Son has a separate *hypostasis*? Doesn't that condemnation amount to endorsing a Sabellian view?"

Hosius realized that he had underestimated Constantine's perceptiveness. "Again, Augustus, these words carry different meanings depending on context. *Hypostasis* can mean 'distinct existence' or it can mean 'substance,' what God is as three or what God is as One. The latter meaning prevails here."

"Then you concede the word *is* ambiguous," Constantine rejoined. "How can we punish someone for refusing to agree to an ambiguous statement? No one who understands the Trinity as referring to three *hypostases* and one *ousia* should be forced to deny that understanding. For I must tell you, Hosius, it is exactly my own!"

"And mine as well. But *hypostasis* and *ousia* are interchangeable when referring to the source of the Son's generation, because the Father is uniquely that source. The Son was not generated from anything else but that source, certainly not out of nothing as the Arians contend. That is the reason for the wording of this section of the anathema."

Although not entirely satisfied by this explanation, Constantine could not articulate an objection to it. Reading consternation in the Emperor's rumpled brow and pursed lips, Hosius promptly turned the discussion away from semantics and to practicalities. "Have you given any thought, Augustus, to the sanctions to be imposed on those who refused to subscribe to the creed?"

"Banishment from their episcopates, I suppose. Thankfully there were only a few dissenters. I am gratified that Eusebius Pamphilus was not among them; he is proof that God's grace can turn a man from error to truth. Eusebius of Nicomedia and Theognis accepted the *homoousios* formulation but rejected the anathema, so their treatment presents a more difficult question. I was inclined to impose some lesser penalty on them given what I saw as ambiguity in the language—if, indeed, that was the reason for their reluctance. But you tell me that the confusion is solely mine. Still, I am disposed toward something more lenient here."

"I think that would be a mistake, my lord. Eusebius in particular remains a danger to the unity we have accomplished. Of all the apostates, he is the most headstrong and outspoken. If we allow him to remain in Nicomedia, we may embolden him to rekindle the controversy."

"Your point is taken. We don't want that."

"Then I must make two further suggestions, Augustus. First, I suggest personal letters from you to all the faithful, expressing your full support for the creed and decrying the Arians in the strongest terms. The church here in Nicomedia should be encouraged in particular to adhere to the faith set out by the council and to elect a bishop who will uphold that faith. Your backing for the creed will be invaluable."

"Indeed, I've been contemplating such letters myself, Hosius, not just to the Nicomedians but to Alexandria, and Caesarea, and other major sees. But it is the bishops themselves who must lead their flocks to the light, and preserve them in unity. I will give whatever support I can. What is your second suggestion?"

"I propose an imperial decree that all copies of Arius's writings are to be destroyed, so that they do not lead others astray and undermine our efforts to curtail this heresy. Any disobedience to this edict must be harshly punished."

"I agree. It shall be done."

The Spaniard paused before asking the question that had been weighing on his mind for some time. "And what is to become of Arius himself?"

"Leave that one to me, Hosius," was Constantine's curt reply. "I am well aware of your contempt for the man. But I have no intentions of making a martyr of him."

"You are most merciful, Augustus."

"Mercy has nothing to do with it. Arius's offense lies in being on the wrong side of the majority, but his challenge was never motivated by malice. For the sacred cause of unity, I am fully committed to supporting the council and declaring his challenge heretical, but my commitment is based on the ecumenical consensus of the church, not on the strength of its logic. Where Scripture is equivocal, I place my faith in God's holy church acting as a body, not in my ability to comprehend all of its theology. Time will tell whether my faith is well placed. Clearly there was something in Arius's arguments that resonated with many, even quieting the Alexandrians at the council. His intellectual challenge remains to be met—intellectually, not by fiat. If there is any kernel of truth in his doctrine, it will germinate despite our best efforts to crush it, for truth has a way of resisting suppression. And if his doctrine is false, it will die out in time. We must wait for that time to pass, and see if it takes root despite our scorching the earth beneath it. But I will not water that earth with his blood!"

Chapter 34

Arius's sparse and tiny prison cell in Nicomedia had a vague air of familiarity. If this was not the precise cell occupied by Lucian of Antioch on the last night of his life, it was at least in the same wing. The accommodations, he noted in the dim light from a tiny barred window, had not improved since his last visit. A wooden cot with some less-than-fresh straw, a small stool, one malodorous chamber pot and several inquisitive mice to keep him company.

The reason for his arrest had not been announced to him. From its timing, he presumed it was related to the ruckus he made at the palace in Nicaea, and not on account of his theological views, which had never yet been declared a crime. Or had they? It did seem strange to him that a local disturbance would not be dealt with locally, without transport from Nicaea to Nicomedia. Perhaps his imprisonment was motivated by both considerations. He would know soon enough; Roman law required that he be charged promptly.

Evening finally brought a meager meal, and then a visitor he relished more than the food: Eusebius of Nicomedia. The two embraced with tears welling in their eyes.

Arius was full of questions for his old friend, who patiently recounted the events of the day to the dejected presbyter, reciting the newly adopted creed to his friend verbatim. "In the end, the memory of Antioch was too fresh for some, the promise of imperial favor too alluring for others; we never had a fair chance," the bishop finally commented. "Hosius played it masterfully, letting us provide the template for a creed and then challenging only the controversial points. Constantine himself added *homoousios* to

Chapter 34

the mix—as if he even knew what he was talking about! It went essentially unchallenged."

"Did no one protest that the word is unscriptural?"

"No one. What would have been the point? It was already obvious at that stage that there could be but one result acceptable to the majority, and there was little sentiment among our group for challenging the Emperor. Many, myself included, simply decided that the word was ambiguous enough to accept, although I think it was deliberately chosen in an effort to separate us from the Alexandrians. The vote was nearly unanimous; even Pamphilus signed the creed. I refused to agree to the anathema, but could see no reason to court excommunication by rejecting the creed itself. Perhaps I am to be excommunicated anyway, for failing to condemn your views explicitly. We shall see. Thus far, that honor is bestowed only on you."

"So, that much has been decided?"

"A foregone conclusion. The anathema assures it."

"Will I be exiled, then?"

Eusebius drew his stool closer and took the Libyan's hand in his own. "I suppose so. But wherever you end up, we will stay in touch, my friend. I have no intention of ending my support for the cause of truth. And I will bide my time as long as I must."

The two men fell quiet for a time, each contemplating an uncertain future. At last Eusebius changed the topic. "Tell me; what did Constantina want of you?"

"She gave me something of urgent importance, something I then tried to deliver to you at the council, without success. It seems that Hosius and Constantine mean to alter the Epistle of John!"

The bishop stared blankly back at Arius, who explained what he had seen. "Constantina handed me a copy of a papyrus containing the final verses of the Epistle in Greek, which she found in Constantine's chambers. It was taken from me when I was locked in this cell, or I would show it to you now. It has marginal notations in Latin, she believes in Hosius' handwriting. Where the Greek states 'There are three that testify: the Spirit and the water and the blood, and these three agree,' Hosius crossed it out and inserted 'There are three that testify: the Father, the Word, and the Holy Spirit, and these three are one.' And then there is a further notation, 'Let the copyists include this change.' I tried to put this revisionist plot into your hands before the vote, but Constantine's guards would not admit me to the assembly. I thought, perhaps, that if you disclosed this attempted alteration

151

of Scripture to the council there might be sufficient outrage to persuade some to change their votes."

Eusebius' face grew ashen as he assimilated what he had just heard. "Remarkable! But I doubt that presenting this at the council would have swayed anyone. There is no unequivocal indication of a wide-ranging conspiracy in this, however suspicious the note about the copyists may be. Nothing would have been gained by raising the matter, I assure you; no one in that hall was prepared to think the worst of the Emperor and his advisor, much less voice an accusation. They all feared retribution. And besides, who would believe that Hosius and Constantine are foolish enough to presume that they could ever succeed in such a plan to revise the epistle? Too many copies of it are already in existence, and many more quotations of its original ending may be found in the writings of various church fathers. Surely they cannot all be revised or destroyed!"

"I suppose you are right about that," Arius sighed. "Yet I have seen alternative versions of Scripture before, and hesitate to explain them all as the innocent errors of overworked scribes who mistook someone else's marginal note as a part of the original. I have learned not to underestimate these trinitarians. There are zealots among them who would have no qualms about passing off their doctrine as scriptural. In Caesarea not very long ago, I was shown by Eusebius Pamphilus an ancient version of Matthew's gospel which ended with the words 'Go therefore and make disciples of all nations, baptizing them in my name,' and someone had stricken out 'my name' and inserted 'in the name of the Father and of the Son and of the Holy Spirit' in the margin. Pamphilus himself took the shorter version to be the authentic one, and quoted it in several of his writings. I have ever since shared his suspicion that Matthew indeed wrote 'my name' originally, and some enterprising scribe changed it to express the trinitarian formulation and then managed to give his new copy wide circulation."

"Come now, Arius! Unless this supposed scheme was hatched quite early, before many copies of the gospel existed, the success of such a venture would require a conspiracy of major proportions; all of the manuscripts with the shorter ending would need to be rounded up and suppressed as well. And if your Caesarean manuscript were *that* old, surely it predated any theological push to clarify the nature of the Son's relationship to the Father. Let's not forget that Father, Son and Holy Spirit have been invoked and confessed together since the beginnings of the church, not only in baptisms but in catechetical instruction, in exorcisms, in preaching, in hymns and

Chapter 34

prayers, even in the blessing at the end of Paul's second letter to the Corinthians that has long been used in our Eucharistic services—well before any theological debates broke out over what these three are in relationship to each other. Isn't it far more likely that what you saw in Caesarea was simply someone's correction of a spurious shortened version back to Matthew's original wording?"

"Is it? No similar expression incorporating this triplet in connection with baptism is found anywhere else in our gospels and epistles. Without exception, all of the other baptismal formulas found in these holy texts are in tension with Matthew's triune commission—prime among them being the passage in the second chapter of the Acts of the Apostles, where Peter admonishes the first converts to 'Repent, and be baptized every one of you in the name of Jesus Christ, so that your sins may be forgiven.' No trinitarian formulation there! And then there are the references in Paul's letters to the Romans, to the Corinthians and to the Galatians suggesting that it is solely in the name of Christ that we are to be baptized. These passages show us how the early church conducted its baptisms—in *one* name, not three! Is it reasonable to assume that Christ added two additional names in his baptismal commission to his apostles, when these other passages unanimously tell us that those apostles then followed a very different tradition? Is it reasonable to think that on that first Pentecost, at his very first public proclamation, Peter would ignore Christ's final instructions and disobey him *again*?"

Eusebius remained skeptical. "What of the baptismal instruction found in the Teaching of the Twelve Apostles? '*Concerning baptism, you should baptize this way: After first explaining all things, baptize in the name of the Father, and of the Son, and of the Holy Spirit, in flowing water.*'"

"Few scholars consider the Teaching of the Twelve Apostles authoritative, Eusebius, and none suggest that the original apostles held to all of its tenets, despite its title. Perhaps the Teaching simply followed a local tradition based on the altered Matthew, and ignored the other Scriptural evidence. This kind of alteration can happen, my friend. It can be *made* to happen, by one as powerful as Constantine."

"I think you are being somewhat paranoid here, Arius. Even an emperor cannot add to the word of God!"

"Ah, but isn't that exactly what he has just done in Nicaea?"

The two men stared at each other in silence.

Chapter 35

By land and sea, our return to Alexandria after the council wrapped up its remaining business took six arduous weeks. Alexander, though jubilant with the result, was exhausted from the ordeal. I see just how much the contest took out of him, sapping his strength and wrecking his health. He is showing his years.

Perhaps he knows his time is drawing near, for he speaks often of the qualities needed for his successor. I dare not ask whether the praises he lavishes on me for embodying those very qualities are an indication that has *me* in mind for the post, but if there is a short list of those likely to garner his support, I believe I am on it. He has ordained me as a presbyter and sends me regularly to preach throughout the Nile delta, as though he intends for me to survey the limits of the episcopate overseen from Alexandria. The prospect of succeeding him as bishop both elates and terrifies me. Yet such a powerful pulpit would be an invaluable aid to accomplishing the work I still feel called to accomplish: continuing the fight against heresy.

The fight is far from over. Widespread promulgation of the Nicene creed has not put the Arian heresy to rest by any stretch. Constantine wrote to all the churches after the council ended that "*every question received due and full examination, until that judgment which God, who sees all things, could approve, and which tended to unity and concord, was brought to light, so that no room was left for further discussion or controversy in relation to the faith.*" Hardly! Doubts linger in the minds of many, perhaps even including the Emperor himself. Two of the four bishops who were excommunicated in the aftermath of Nicaea, including Eusebius of Nicomedia, are rumored to have petitioned Constantine for permission to return to their sees, and

Chapter 35

he in turn is rumored to be favorably disposed to their petitions. The *homoousios* formulation has proven to be a far more fluid concept than any of us had anticipated; allegiances to it are sworn, but the beliefs of the clerics so swearing are varied, shaded. I find myself still defending against challenges to the consubstantiality of Father and Son, even here in Alexandria. And once Alexander passes on, this is bound to increase.

Nevertheless, the struggle for the hearts and minds of Christians throughout the empire is bearing fruit among the many common worshippers who now profess adherence to the creed. Even in Baucalis where Arius's heresy thrived for years, more and more congregants are accepting the Nicene teaching as authoritative. For the vast majority of simple believers, there is something inherently legitimate in a doctrinal statement sanctioned by so many bishops. The uneducated masses who cannot comprehend the nuances of the Trinity naturally rely on the wisdom of teachers they deem wiser than themselves. But for how long? Unless they appreciate at least its basic concept, their conception of the three-in-One will remain vulnerable to heresies. It falls upon the orthodox clergy to maintain the momentum produced by the synod, and preserve it from the attacks still being mounted against its decrees. We must provide the "rational explanation for an irrational concept" that Arius challenged us to provide at Nicaea.

That is my challenge; that is my mission.

In my own preaching I search for analogies that may, in some small way, help to explain the Trinity. Always they fall short. But today, returning from a week of preaching in Memphis, I have finally found one. When I wasn't even trying. I see now that it had to happen that way. Years of attaining to theological insight by my own initiative, whether through intellectual effort or meditative endeavor, had proved time and again to be futile, proved that I wasn't ready to receive it. I was asking my soul to reason, when it simply needed to invite. Somewhere in the prayerful solitude of his hermitage, blessed Anthony surely must be smiling—for I have finally taken his counsel, tempering my self-reliance, opening myself to God's capacity to impart understanding on *His* timetable rather than mine. And He has poured out His Spirit to guide my path.

Particularly in summer when the hot desert air thins and rises, the cooler, heavier air at the surface of the Mediterranean is sucked south to replace it, creating a breeze strong enough for ships to sail up the Nile against the current. But it also slows navigation downriver. When I awoke this morning, the wind was as robust as I have ever encountered, prompting my decision to return home on horseback rather than by boat.

The land route from Memphis to Alexandria passes by way of Giza, where the urge to tarry awhile at the pyramids is almost irresistible. I succumb to it willingly. Viewing these awesome structures, ancient tombs of the Pharaohs, I can only guess what secrets are buried within. As I stand spellbound in front of the massive pyramid of Cheops, the largest in the necropolis, it is impossible to tell whether the structure has four sides or three, whether its base is a square or a triangle. From my perspective, my frame of reference, only one face of the pyramid is visible; the others can be neither counted nor measured. I imagine it as a tetrahedron, a triangular base resting on the earth with three sides rising to a peak above.

Suddenly, as if a door had opened in front of me and I was passed through it weightlessly by an unseen force without moving my feet, I am drawn into the presence of the great pyramid. It seems to grow exponentially taller in front of me, filling my senses to the exclusion of everything else. I am overcome by illumination, a pervasive light without identifiable source, like the light that first afternoon in Nicaea. The pyramid before me is somehow even more luminous, delineated within the light, dominating my consciousness, shining like the sun. Shining like the face of Christ at his transfiguration.

The face of God!

Could understanding the Trinity really be as simple as this? Each of the three "persons" in one God is not a person in the ordinary sense of denoting a distinct individual, but a *persona* in the sense of a portrayal or a posture, an outward-looking manifestation of an inward unity. The Greek word *prosōpon* expresses this rather well—an actor's mask, a character, a face. I encounter Father, or Son, or Holy Spirit, depending on which face is facing me. The three "persons" are *relational*; they are distinct realities of the one God in relation to me, in relation to humanity, in relation to the created universe.

It all fits. The *prosōpon* of God that Exodus recounts as one no man may see and live is not the same *prosōpon* that is elsewhere described in Scripture as beneficial, even salvific. There, in the fourth chapter of Genesis: "Cain said to the Lord, 'My punishment is greater than I can bear! Today you have driven me away from the soil, and I shall be hidden from your face.'" There, in the sixth chapter of Numbers: "The Lord bless you and keep you; the Lord make his face to shine upon you, and be gracious to you; the

Chapter 35

Lord lift up his countenance upon you, and give you peace." There, in the eightieth Psalm: "Restore us, O God; let your face shine, that we may be saved." Beholding *this* face of God is not life-ending, but life-*saving*. The distinction turns on the relation of facer to faced, on which face of the Godhead is turned toward us. Yet distinct realities each of them must be, for if they were identical their effects on us would be identical as well.

The one God's triune nature persists in each of these three faces, as inseparable from each other as are the sides of a pyramid. In that very unity lies their shared essence. It is not a material essence, not shared as the faces of a pyramid share the same core of stone, eliminating any real distinction of substance comprising the sides. That is where Sabellius went wrong, analogizing to the material world and supposing the common "stuff" of the divine to be the defining substance of a single entity. No, the shared essence of these three persons lies in *what they form* in their unity, as the joining together of triangles edge to edge with a common apex forms the shape we know as a pyramid. It is "pyramidness" itself, not what the pyramid as a solid might be made of, that constitutes this essence. And so it is with the Godhead. We can never fully comprehend the divine "stuff" of the Godhead; that is beyond our power to describe through analogies to the physical world. But the concept of God, like the abstract concept of a three-sided pyramid, is revealed by the particular relation, the particular union, of its distinct faces. Without the three, there is not the One.

What is not material cannot be apprehended by the physical senses, impeding recognition of our encounters with God. Yet I am gripped by the certainty that we are meant to encounter God face to face. To be hidden from his face, to be outside his presence, is truly to be in exile. Cain knew this all too well; in anguish he "went away from the presence of the Lord, and settled in the land of Nod, east of Eden." Wherever that mythical place of banishment may lie, on earth or in our very souls, humanity yearns for a return to the garden, to the dazzling light of the face of God. How, then, do we find it? How are we to recognize the way, limited as we are by our human nature, imprisoned in a material world? This is the problem we cannot solve on our own; God must solve it for us.

And He has.

John tells us both that no one has ever seen God and that whoever has seen the Son has seen the Father. There is no contradiction; it *is* possible for human nature to see the face of God in His image. It *is* possible for human nature to see the face of the *incarnate* God. And that is John's point. That

Heresy

is the point of the divine taking on flesh, to reveal itself to flesh. That is the point of Paul's message to the Corinthians, "For it is the God who said, 'Let light shine out of darkness,' who has shone in our hearts to give the light of the knowledge of the glory of God in the face of Jesus Christ."

Yes, the *face* of Jesus Christ! His, we can see! He is the visible embodiment of God, as the Father is the mind of God and the Spirit is the soul of God. Mind, body and soul, a trinity of indivisible unity, each facet in relation to the whole, and to the whole of creation, seen through the body visible but not divisible. It is the Son, the second facet of this blessed unity, who reaches out to our humanity frozen in awe of the ineffable Supreme Being, and invites us to walk with him, to walk around the pyramid that is the Godhead and behold the face of the invisible Father—and *live*! It is the Holy Spirit, the third facet, who enters into the quiet recesses of our hearts and guides us to the Father.

These three are inseparable. These three are one.

The sun sinks in the western sky, and the pyramids of Giza cast lengthening shadows across the silent desert sand.

www.ingramcontent.com/pod-product-compliance
Lightning Source LLC
Chambersburg PA
CBHW051103160426
43193CB00010B/1293